# PECK'S BEACH

## A Pictorial History of
# OCEAN CITY, NJ

*Tim Cain*

DOWN THE SHORE / The SandPaper
PUBLISHING

WEST CREEK, NEW JERSEY

Much of the material in this book has been adapted from a series of columns that appeared in the Ocean City edition of *The SandPaper* during 1987. This book was originally published in 1988, with several printings in hardcover and softcover, in slightly different form.

**DOWN THE SHORE** / **The SandPaper**
PUBLISHING

The words "Down The Shore" and the Down The Shore Publishing logo is a registered U.S. Trademark.

Down The Shore Publishing Corp.
Box 100, West Creek, N.J. 08092

**www.down-the-shore.com**

Book design by Leslee Ganss
Printed in China
4 6 8 10 9 7 5 3

Revised edition, 2016.
ISBN 978-0-945582-04-5

Library of Congress Cataloging-in-Publication Data

Cain, Tim, 1949 -
Peck's Beach
Bibliography: p.
Includes index.
1. Ocean City (N.J.) — History.  2. Methodist Church — New Jersey — Ocean City — History.
3. Ocean City (N.J.) — Description — Views.  4. Ocean City (N.J.) — Church History.  I. Title.
F144.015C35  1988   974.9'98        88-11871
ISBN 0-945582-00-5 (pbk.)
ISBN 0-945582-04-8 (hdcvr.)

A.M.D.G.

# Contents

Readers should note that these pages were written in the late 1980s. Although a few references may have changed, the remarkable history of "America's Greatest Family Resort" — the barrier island once known as Peck's Beach — remains as true as ever.

*Early beach scenes: A beached whale became an irresistable photo opportunity, and the attraction of the surf in summer (looking north from 13th Street) is timeless, facing page.*

*On the boardwalk behind the Flanders Hotel, Joseph Champion, a mayor from early in the 20th century, points to the motto that has served Ocean City well through the years.*

# *Foreword*

Ocean City, N.J. is a city founded on religious principles, but which has changed its character gradually over more than a century so that it could keep in step with changes in public customs and perceptions.

Having written two books about the early years of Ocean City, I know first-hand how difficult it is to get an unvarnished view of how things used to be. As a newspaperman, I grew accustomed to working against deadlines, and consequently my first book was written in haste so as to be available during the second summer of our Historical Museum's existence. Thus I can only admire the hard work, perseverance and ingenuity of the writer of this book to bring the reader a more comprehensive review of the city's background.

Old-timers are a great resource. Their observations fascinate us because the island once was so different. However, much information about earlier times must be gathered from old newspaper accounts, letters, diaries, public records and other such sources. Such items exist, but are not always easy to find.

Ocean City has been undergoing change almost from its inception, and those changes are still going on. Anyone who was here at or about the turn of the century would not even recognize the place today. Even in my own limited experience it becomes difficult to recall what used to be at a certain location. After a century of growth, there is relatively little physical evidence remaining from the early days. Here and there are old buildings that have withstood time, but many have been razed, burned down, or were victims of storms and replaced by newer structures. What used to be bare land is now occupied by duplex apartments or motels. In short, we have become an island of lost landmarks.

As you peruse this book, you will come to see that it is Ocean City's subdued atmosphere that has attracted so many families here for, in some cases, three generations. Unfortunately, most of the people holding influential positions in the city today were not here during the formative years, so it is healthy to have a publication such as this to remind them of the how and why of Ocean City.

As one who has a lifelong interest, I can only hope that readers will gain a greater understanding of the community, and maybe even figure out why they came here in the first place.

*Harold Lee*
*Ocean City, NJ*
*1988*

*A 1903 map of Ocean City promotes the amenities of the town, which was then less than a quarter-century old.*

# *Introduction*

The history of Ocean City is, like the story of America itself, one of contradictions. It is about an island whose beautiful environment can turn deadly any time a bad storm sweeps up the coast. It is about an ocean that gives and *yet* also takes away. It is a tale about Methodist ministers who dreamed of establishing a Christian colony at the shore and real estate developers who dreamed of making their fortunes here. It is about quiet Sundays amidst the hustle and bustle of a resort town. And it's about change — and a resistance to change.

Before the late 19th century, the island called Peck's Beach and later renamed Ocean City was a rugged, sandy clump of earth jutting out into the Atlantic, overgrown with bayberry, cedar trees and shrubs, and hosting wild cattle and hogs that made it a hunter's paradise. Within a little more than 100 years it has become a pleasant, fully developed resort town with an atmosphere that has made it attractive to residents and vacationers alike.

How it became what it is today is the subject of this book. The characters who played a role in the development of the city and its history are as varied and distinct from one another as one can imagine. The Lake brothers, for instance, who sought to start a Christian revival center and ended up founding a town, were men of vision and shrewd business sense. The often nameless, avant-garde individuals who broke with tradition and custom moved the community toward modernity. And, of course, Ocean City's own royal family, the Kellys, brought vigor and glamour to their summer home.

The memories and writings of people who have visited or resided on the island in past years, or who have found its history as fascinating as I have, were immeasurably helpful in making this book a reality. A wealth of information, myths and photographs were made available to me by many generous people. Thanks to all of them.

*Tim Cain*
*Ocean City, NJ*
*1988*

*Something about the Shore has always inspired people to pose for pictures, from the earliest cameras to selfies. Here, bathers, boardwalk strollers, fishermen, and beach gals with parasols all delight in documenting their time in Ocean City.*

*The boardwalk at 9th Street in 1925.*

The Sindia, *shortly after it grounded in December 1901.*

*An excercise class on the beach in 1923.*

*Fast friends, early 1920s.*

# CHAPTER ONE

# Native Americans:
# The First Summer Visitors

About 12,000 years ago, a people known as Paleo-Indians lived in coastal New Jersey. These hunter-gatherers are believed to have migrated here along major rivers, and their relics have been found among the bones of the enormous mammals identified with the Ice Age. Then, about 4,000 years later, several millennia before the Trojan War, they left.

For the following 5,000 years, the Atlantic seaboard was sparsely populated, until the migration of the Woodland Indians into the region, sometime between the reign of the Biblical King David and the building of the second temple in Jerusalem in about 1000 B.C.

It was during this time that the sea rose to its present level. When the Paleo-Indians had come into the region, the coastline was 100 miles east of where it is now. Melting glaciers gradually submerged what these early Americans knew as the oceanfront.

The Lenni-Lenape Indians were the first residents of what is now

> *During the warmer seasons, the tribesmen traveled across the bay to the island. Like today's summer residents and visitors, the Lenni-Lenape fished, crabbed, gathered shellfish, and swam the foamy waters of the ocean surf.*

southern New Jersey to discover the attractiveness of the island we know as Ocean City, using it as a fishing ground. Though native Americans, they were settlers in the region — a western tribe that had migrated to the area hundreds of years before European explorers arrived from the east.

The local Lenni-Lenape tribe called itself the Tuckahoe and resided on the mainland, where they built lodges in which they lived most of the year. The Indians were great hunters and fishermen; and the area was perfect for both endeavors. Furthermore, the rich agricultural land brought forth an abundance of fruit and vegetables to complement their diet.

During the warmer seasons, the tribesmen traveled across the bay to the island. Like today's summer residents and visitors, the Lenni-Lenape fished, crabbed, gathered shellfish, and swam the foamy waters of the ocean surf. Then, as temperatures dropped, they returned to the mainland for harvesting their crops and hunting game, which would be preserved and eaten throughout the winter.

The first Europeans the Indians encountered were as

*The Lenni-Lenape spent the warmer seasons on New Jersey's barrier islands including Peck's Beach. These illustrations from the 1854 book* American Family Robinson *were reprinted in the early 1900s in* Heston's Annals of Absegami.

peaceful as they. The Quakers, or Friends, whom William Penn led to this part of the country believed in fair treatment of the indigenous populations.

Unlike many other Christian settlers in the New World, Quakers believed that the Indians too possessed "that of God" in them and therefore were worthy of respect. Penn insisted that his fellow Quakers pay for lands they wished to appropriate and that they only establish settlements where the native inhabitants welcomed them. For these reasons the region lacks a history of Indian-European hostility found in other parts of the Americas.

As in Pennsylvania, to which the majority of Quakers immigrated, the settlement of the mainland across from the island was part of what Penn called his "Holy Experiment," an attempt to demonstrate that it was possible to create a society free of wars and other attendant ills of the Old World. Records of this period also praise the Lenni-Lenape as friendlier and more honest than neighboring tribes.

Nevertheless, even though they enjoyed good relations with

*Unlike many other Christian settlers in the New World, Quakers believed that the Indians too possessed "that of God" in them and therefore were worthy of respect. Penn insisted that his fellow Quakers pay for lands they wished to appropriate and that they only establish settlements where the native inhabitants welcomed them.*

their newly arrived neighbors, the Tuckahoe pushed west in 1692, feeling crowded and anticipating the larger waves of immigrants from Europe that lay ahead.

# CHAPTER TWO

# Early European Settlers

*This 1698 map of "Pennsylvania and West Jersey," from* Heston's Annals of Absegami, *calls Ocean City "Some Wood Land, Some Sandy Ground."*

Perhaps the first European to note his discovery of the island was David Pieterzen De Vries, a Dutch explorer who described it as "flat sand beaches with low hills." It was first surveyed in 1695 by a Burlington, N.J., man, Thomas Budd, who sold it to Pennsylvanian John Somers that year.

Budd's survey followed his purchase of large tracts of land that included property on the mainland, along with the island now called Ocean City, and the portion of Absecon Island later to become Atlantic City. Ironically, Budd was forced by the agreement of sale with the West Jersey Society to buy the strands in order to take possession of the mainland sites that were the object of his land speculation. For the rich agricultural property on the mainland, Budd paid forty cents an acre, while he bought the seemingly useless island properties for four cents an acre.

Referring to what is now Atlantic City, Budd told the surveyor general, "I don't want that swampland at any price. It will never be good for anything but seagull nests."

Budd used the island of Ocean City for grazing cattle and harvesting bayberry, sassafras and other herbs for sale to Holland and its European neighbors.

During the period that Budd used the island for his cattle, others were using the site as a lookout for hunting whales. One such man was a whaler by the name of John Peck, who operated from the island in the late 17th and early 18th centuries. While not much is known about him, his existence on the island is documented in a Burlington, N.J., court record from 1700. It cites a lawsuit naming Peck as having legal ownership of a whale stranded upon the beach where he worked.

Around the turn of the century, the island began to be referred to as Peck's Beach, and it is probable the name came from John Peck.

Since deeds of the time often were haphazardly registered, acreage sometimes was sold to more than one person, and so it happened that Richard Townsend of Cape May County bought 663 acres of Peck's Beach in 1726. Townsend, too, used the land for cattle grazing and willed it to his sons Samuel and Daniel in 1737.

*This survey, dated February 12, 1753, deeded Richard Somers part of the island then called Peck's Beach.*

*Although known as a "dry" town, Ocean City has in its history been home to some revelry.*

Histories differ on the means by which cattle and hogs were transported to Peck's Beach. Some tell of flatboats ferrying the animals across the bay, while others insist that the cattle, at least, were made to swim and wade the Great Egg Harbor Bay. According to some accounts, the progeny of these domestic farm animals soon reverted to their wild state, and by the time of the American Revolution, parties of farmers and adventurers alike often would cross over to the island to hunt for pork or beef. A small herd of untamed cattle still inhabited the uncultivated place more than 100 years later when a group of ministers founded Ocean City.

The beach also became a favorite site for less sober activities. Many young people considered the secluded tract a perfect retreat for celebrations, especially those featuring drinking bouts. Accordingly, what is now Ocean City came to be known as "Party Island." The sexes would separate to bathe, reflecting the mores of the 17th and 18th centuries, but would rejoin for dancing, drinking, and festivities which sometimes included peculiar party games. One custom was for the young men to carry women to

Another claimant to the island was Richard Somers, who inherited part of the island and bought another 550 acres from the West Jersey Society in 1750. His will of 1752 contains the first mention of a structure on the island.

As Budd's attitude illustrates, at the time of the earliest settlement of Europeans on the mainland, the island was considered of little value. The sandy soil, overgrown brush and cedar swamps on the island held little appeal for the pragmatic farmers who tilled the fertile soil across the bay. However, the natural boundaries of water made the beach a practical grazing land for animals, and, among others, Thomas Budd, Richard Townsend and Richard Somers all used the island for that purpose.

*The waters surrounding Peck's Beach made it an excellent natural corral for pasturing cattle.*

the top of the hill, bind their feet, and roll them down to the edge of the surf.

Some revelers would bring cats along to their beach parties and, inevitably, descendants of the abandoned domestic felines soon developed characteristics of their ancestors, wildly roaming the island in search of prey.

Other visitors to Peck's Beach included scavengers. As with the other barrier islands to the north and south, the beach was the site of shipwrecks and groundings — occasions for both noble rescues and profitable lootings.

Custom dictated that the first person to reach a ship abandoned by its crew could lay claim to its cargo. With shipwrecks a common event, mainlanders always kept a keen eye out for the opportunity to salvage.

In addition to the natural hazards of navigating in coastal waters, ships often were lured into the shallows by land pirates eager to strip them clean. Unscrupulous scavengers would tie a lantern to the tail of a cow or mule and then leave the animal loose to wander the beach. Storm-battered crews, according to legend, would mistake the light for that of a passing vessel, steer toward it, and find themselves stranded. Once abandoned, such ships' treasures were easy pickings.

# CHAPTER THREE

# Parker Miller: The Original Year-Round Resident

"Any port in a storm" was calamitous advice to captains sailing the South Jersey coast in the 18th and 19th centuries. Though sailors could count on rescue aid should their ships founder off Peck's Beach, they could be just as certain that their vessels' bounty would be looted should they wreck or run aground. To counter this activity, the first permanent resident of Peck's Beach, Parker Miller, was sent to the island in the 1850s.

Miller was an agent for marine insurance companies, hired to deter thieves and to protect the legal interests of the shipping merchants. Using the remains of the wrecked English barge *Dashaway* for construction materials, he and his family built the first real home on the island just south of the corner of 7th Street and Asbury Avenue›.

With a wife and six children, Miller's family comprised the first little community on Peck's Beach, and two of those children, Amy and Simeon, were the first to be born on the island. Besides his duties as agent for maritime concerns, Miller farmed the sandy soil and raised cattle. When his son Walter matured, Parker assisted him with his bayside fishery and clam and oyster beds.

The Miller home was no hermitage, though. Large numbers of hunters, attracted to the island by an abundance of game, including deer, ducks, geese, wild cats and cattle, sought and found accommodations with the genial Millers. Some of the wild cattle the sportsmen hunted were actually part of Miller's herd that had

*Parker Miller was the island's first recorded year-round resident.*

wandered away and joined with other strays of farmers who also used the island as a grazing pasture. This untamed, roaming herd numbered about thirty by the time the Lake brothers, founders of the city, arrived on the island, and the animals became so wild that not even Miller could safely approach them.

In 1881, two years after the Ocean City Association was formed, minutes of one of its meetings recount that "Miller and others" were leased "a piece of ground on the lower end of the beach for $1, to be used to erect a pen for the capture of cattle now on the beach."

Nevertheless, attempts to bring the herd into captivity were fruitless until one day, seven years later. The men of Ocean City organized a posse to gun down the wild bunch. From 7:00 a.m. until mid-morning, rifle-toting men swept the south end of the island in a hunt that would have done Buffalo Bill Cody proud. When the smoke cleared, carcasses of bulls, cows and calves gave testimony to the resolve of the townsfolk to rid themselves of the dangerous animals.

One huge bull remained, however. The "boss of the herd" witnesses called him. For about nine hours the hardy animal eluded and deflected bullets and shotgun pellets like a creature from a horror film. A few members of the hunting party claimed that they had been chased up trees or galloped over by the fiendish beast. Others said that they had let loose their shot with both barrels at close range and still narrowly escaped the treacherous horns. Only a bullet shot directly through its heart was able to bring the bull down, and down he came, all 900 pounds of him. At four o'clock in the afternoon the sovereign bovine lay dead, the greatest and last of the wild cattle of Peck's Beach.

*The home of Parker Miller offered hospitality to hunters and visitors to the island.*

# CHAPTER FOUR

# An Irish Recluse and a Providential Survey

Conflict over land claims sparked a series of events that eventually led to the creation of a Christian retreat on Peck's Beach. Although insurance claims agent Parker Miller and his family lived virtually alone on the island in the last quarter of the 19th century, Miller found himself defending his property rights in 1872.

Five years earlier he had purchased a tract of land from his landlord, Jesse Somers, but the exact dimensions of Somers' holdings came under dispute and ended up in Cape May County Court. A commission was created to determine the boundary lines of the property owned by Jesse and other of his relatives.

The land was divided into eight parts, seven of which were allotted to members of the Somers family and one to Miller. A report in 1873 specified that Parker Miller received the land on which his house, barn and windmill were built. However, both Miller and Jesse Somers were dissatisfied with the commission's rulings, and they consequently hired a surveyor from Bargaintown to recheck the boundaries according to the terrain. His work led to the settlement of their claims.

That surveyor was William Lake, cousin to the brothers who, a few years later, would create the Ocean City Association in an effort to emulate Ocean Grove, a Christian retreat center in Monmouth County to the north. The Lake brothers, who first considered establishing their project in what is now Margate,

*Robert Fisher, the second year-round resident on the island.*

*Robert Fisher's office and twin cottages, at 7th Street and Wesley Avenue, circa 1894. Despite his desire for peaceful isolation, Fisher lived to see Ocean City developed into a bustling town and he shared in its growing prosperity.*

would later see William's surveying work at Peck's Beach as providential.

The Rev. S. Wesley Lake and his colleague, the Rev. William B. Wood, visited the town of Ocean Grove in 1879, ten years after its founding, and were favorably impressed with the theocratic society they found there.

Governed by the Methodist Camp Meeting Association, Ocean Grove's strict religious laws were enforced through the tight control the association held over the land, which was leased rather than deeded to tenants. Each lease carried with it a clause forbidding the sale of alcohol, and the Sunday closing laws were implemented by locking the gates to the town so that no one could enter or leave save by foot.

Lake and Wood were fascinated by the experiment at Ocean Grove and decided to establish a similar resort, with some modifications. Lake talked over the idea with his brothers, Ezra and James, and the three approached their father, Simon, who agreed to mortgage his Pleasantville farm to finance the potentially profitable venture.

Although Simon owned property at the Margate site, adjacent land belonged to others too young to sign a contract of sale. When the Lakes began to investigate other similar areas, they were told by their cousin William about Peck's Beach. Through his surveying of the island, William had come to know both the terrain and the property owners well, and his enthusiasm for the place was evident.

Around the same time, a man named Robert Fisher, from Ulster, Ireland, joined Parker Miller as the second year-round resident on the island. Fisher's real name was William R. F. Thompson, and he assumed his alias for the same reason that he moved to Peck's Beach — to achieve solitude as a means of relief for a nervous condition. Extracts from William Lake's diary indicate that Fisher was a "direct descendant of the Earl of Hume, through his mother, educated at the Royal Irish Academy, Belfast, came to the United States in 1868, [and] was a wine agent for Dunnelle & Co."

> *"Snakes were among the things we calculated on having trouble with, but the trouble did not materialize very seriously…. Very few snakes were encountered as it appeared that some Irish earth had been brought on the Island at some earlier period, and as Saint Patrick had made it death to snakes wherever he came, they are supposed to have taken the hint and gone over to Atlantic [City] where everything was welcome, and seeing snakes no novelty."*

The Lakes hired Fisher to trim away brush and chop down trees as part of a three- or four-man work force employed to make possible William's job of re-surveying the island. Fisher himself kept a diary, with the aspiration of writing a history of the emerging town, and William Lake quoted extensively from Fisher's notes in his own narrative.

Although historians rely on Fisher's writing as a source of facts about the establishment of Ocean City, the man's wit also commends his diary to the reader: "Snakes were among the things we calculated on having trouble with, but the trouble did not materialize very seriously…. Very few snakes were encountered as it appeared that some Irish earth had been brought on the Island at some earlier period, and as Saint Patrick had made it death to snakes wherever he came, they are supposed to have taken the hint and gone over to Atlantic [City] where everything was welcome, and seeing snakes no novelty."

But it is the writer's grace of style that is most striking. His sensitivity as an observer is revealed in his description of the pristine landscape he encountered here: "Seldom in such small compass is such magnificence and variety of scenery displayed and when the sun, gliding westerly to his chamber, bathed it in a gold flood, it formed a picture of enhancing beauty, and the glory of it thrilled the soul, and the intangible telephone established clear connection with the Divine Author."

With the development of the town, Fisher lost his peaceful isolation, but he fared well among his new neighbors, becoming a prosperous real estate and insurance broker as well as a notary public, and later serving the town as its mayor and a member of City Council.

# CHAPTER FIVE

# The Reverends Lake and The Town's Genesis

On September 10, 1879, the Reverends James, Wesley and Ezra Lake and their old friend, the Rev. William H. Burrell, landed a small sailing craft on the bay side of Peck's Beach. The clergymen had traveled the waterways from Pleasantville to look over the island that the Lakes' cousin William had recommended to them.

In their hearts and minds was the hope that this would be the site God had chosen for them to found a Christian resort and camp meeting ground. They walked up a northerly cowpath to a high bluff, and, after taking in a panorama of the island, they knelt beneath a cedar tree to ask God's will in the matter. That tree stood at the corner of Sixth Street and Asbury Avenue into the 1990s and remains a symbol of the values and dreams of the ministers who would later found Ocean City.

A bronze plaque on the site commemorates the event. It names the four men, bears the date of their visit, and concludes, "Honorable Simon Lake and Reverend William B. Wood joined them in incorporating the Ocean City Association October 20, 1879." It was on that date that a formal meeting was called, naming the Lake patriarch, Simon, president of the corporation and renaming Peck's Beach

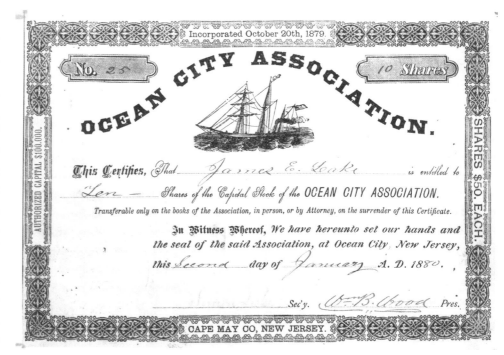

*The Reverends James Lake, left, and his home at 5th Street and Wesley Avenue, and Ezra Lake, right. The certificate for 10 shares of capital stock in the Ocean City Association (facing page) bears the signature of Simon Lake, patriarch of the town's founding family.*

New Brighton. The first corporate members included Simon, Wesley, Ezra and James Lake, as well as the Reverends Burrell and Wood.

A third meeting in November resulted in a consensus that the town to be developed should be called Ocean City, indicative of the admiration the association members felt for Ocean Grove, the Christian resort which had inspired their own endeavor. The fervor of the city's founders was highlighted in the *First Annual Report of the President of the Ocean City Association* by Wood in 1880. Under the title, "Our Basis and Objects — Moral and Religious," Wood wrote, "In the providence of God, this magnificent section of land, on the seashore, has been obtained for Christian occupancy. Looking at its peculiar natural advantages, it is wonderful that some keen-sighted worldlings had not long ago secured it. We believe that God had it in reserve, like some other favored spots, for an inheritance of His people, and for real salvation pur-poses."

The founders envisioned a Christian colony separated from the worldly society of the mainland by nature. The Rev. Burrell made this clear in the poem he wrote which serves as a foreword to the report. The anthem-like verse invites those whose minds are *"Sore vex'd with vice by law sustained,/Where passions vile uncheck'd have reigned"* to find refuge in Ocean City."

Providentially, the poem continues:

*"Both bay and ocean aid our cause,/Protecting us by potent laws,/ From man's invading foe;/In their embrace we dwell secure,/With all the blessings they insure,/ And on mankind bestow./Temptations here/ We need not fear,/Nor dread the drunkard's woe."*

Burrell's concern about feared temptations did not spring from prudishness. Other New Jersey shore resorts had gone the way of all flesh and had, in fact, created the reaction that spawned Ocean Grove. The nearby town of Long Branch in the late 1800s had achieved a level of decadence that caused one boastful town official to christen it "The Monte Carlo of America." Gambling houses, a race track and prostitution characterized the wealthy community, frequented by Diamond Jim Brady and other notorious persons. The state would not see the likes of such glitter again until the construction of casinos in Atlantic City in the late 1970s.

While Long Branch became synonymous with loose morals, a wave of evangelism swept over much of the rest of the coastline. Camp meetings were well attended by Christians intent on hearing the powerful voices of contemporary preachers. Ocean Grove, Sea Grove at Cape May Point, Island Heights, Seaside Park, Atlantic Highlands and, with the coming of the Lakes, Ocean City were locations of campground revival meetings.

The Ocean Grove Camp Meeting Association, in 1869, began evangelistic meetings which eventually led to the founding of a Christian community. The association was able to translate its moral principles into conforming behavior by keeping title to all of the land within its domain and leasing parcels to people sympathetic with its aims. Those found in transgression of its strict Sabbath observance or temperance rules lost their leases and were quickly replaced by people desirous of the type of environment achieved by those strictures.

The Ocean City Association took a slightly different tack. Rather than purchasing and leasing its property, it devised a process of cross-deeding, whereby it first legally acquired title to all of the property on the island and then attached its Sabbath and temperance restrictions to the deeds. Land the original owners wanted to keep was deeded back to them with the accompanying restrictions. By this process, new and old property owners were made to accept restrictions prohibiting the manufacture and sale of alcohol and enforcing the closing of all commercial enterprises on Sundays. In this way, the association remained free to sell its land holdings without compromising its goal of establishing a Christian resort community.

The idealistic Christian ministers and laymen saw their vision realized so quickly that they surely felt God had confirmed their faith in the project. In one year's time, they had built thirty five dwellings, one large hotel (the Brighton), ten private stables or barns, and two public bathhouses. Three government-built life-saving stations also were erected in 1880. Extensive street and railroad development was begun; two issues of the island's first newspaper were published; and an application was made for an Ocean City post office.

While the town's rapid growth may have exceeded the expectations of its founders, they believed their success was understandable from the perspective of divine providence. "Our great leading objects have been moral and religious — not secular," Wood wrote. "If God sends us financial success while maintaining moral integrity, we shall accept it thankfully at His hands…. We have moved forward quietly and without ostentation in the past, so let it be in the future. We can trust our enterprise to speak for itself."

# CHAPTER SIX

# *The Tabernacle*

The Ocean City Tabernacle was the first house of worship built on the island. First named the Auditorium, it was erected in 1881 as an open pavilion for the camp revival meetings by the town's clerical founders.

Religious pilgrims flocked to Christian resorts like Ocean City to spend their vacations camping out by the surf and meeting for prayer and preaching in large congregations. The first such meeting in Ocean City was held from August 6 to August 16, 1880, and, according to the *First Annual Report of the President of the Ocean City Association,* was a success.

"Although in the midst of our work of grading and improvement, and unable to make proper preparations for it, we yielded to the persuasion of friends, and arranged for, and held a Camp Meeting, of ten days continuance," the Rev. William B. Wood wrote in the report. "The attendance was as large as could have been expected, under the circumstances. It was estimated that there were a thousand persons present at the Surf Meeting on Sunday, August 15. Rev. William C. Stockton, with his large tabernacle tent, spent the entire time with us and did good service. The meetings were very spiritual and interesting."

Wood's report also noted that a parcel of land was set aside for a campground upon which to hold such services.

"The space allotted to the encampment is 500 feet wide, from the thoroughfare to the ocean, with plenty of tenting ground," Wood stated. "It is contemplated to have all appointments desirable to render the camp meeting a real feast to the thousands who may congregate there for Christian worship. Those coming to tent with them will have every possible facility that will contribute to their comfort. Besides the regular services of the encampment, there will be temperance conventions, anniversaries, and other Christian and philanthropic convocations, fully occupying the season, and making it memorable in interest and profit. No pains will be spared to give Ocean City a series of religious privileges equal to other resorts of kindred character."

It fell to the president of the association to arrange and supervise these meetings and conventions, under the direction of that organization's board of directors. By the end of the first summer season, Wood realized the necessity of putting up a permanent structure to house these activities.

"A suitable Auditorium must be erected for religious services and assemblies," he wrote, and directed that a permanent meeting place be built on the property set aside for a campground — between Fifth and Sixth streets and Asbury and Wesley avenues.

The frame building was dubbed the Auditorium and was completed according to plan by June, 1881. The 80-by-90-foot building at first consisted only of a main platform, altar and choir platform, according to the association's third annual report, but a building to its rear soon was constructed to house Bible class, special services, child care, and ministers' and janitors' rooms.

"There have been suggestions and consultations with reference to inclosing it to protect it from the weather, and for other purposes, but nothing in that direction has yet been determined upon," the report states.

During that year, the property hosted a National Temperance Camp Meeting, a Bible Reading Service and a Woman's Work Service. The latter event was led by a Miss Oliver, who, the report declares, was "the only female pastor in the world," a fact that prompted scrutiny from the association. "She awakened great interest and was listened to with profit," the report recounts. "We found nothing eccentric or peculiar about her. She is an intelligent, pious, devoted young woman; thoroughly convinced it is her duty to preach the gospel, and able to do it."

Tents for visitors were set up on the grounds, which then overlooked the ocean. Although the association gave out plots for free to people who made "proper application in time," sites and tents also could be rented. The organization subsequently built one- and two-room cottages known as association houses, later called salt boxes. A number of these quaint buildings can still be seen on small lots throughout the island.

When the Ocean City Association turned over the governance of the island to secular authorities in 1884, the city's character began to change accordingly. Still, the Auditorium, renamed the Tabernacle, continued to house religious meetings and conventions during the summer seasons.

In 1944, though, disaster struck in the form of a hurricane, which blew out three walls of the building that had been enclosed years before. At the time, services were still under the direction of the Rev. W. Elwell Lake, son of one of the resort's co-founders, the Rev. S. Wesley Lake. The younger Lake had presided over the Tabernacle's activities from 1928 to 1948. Ralph G. Luff was made president of the association at the end of Lake's tenure

*Early pilgrims to camp revival meetings camped in tents near the beach and later in small cottages.*

*The Auditorium — later renamed the Tabernacle — was built on the platform where tent services were first held. A newer structure replaced it in 1957. The cannon from the British brig* Delight, *wrecked in 1779, stood on the grounds until it disappeared in the 1960s.*

and was succeeded upon his death by his son, William G. Luff.

Following the storm, the Tabernacle was rebuilt and remained standing until 1957, when it was replaced by the larger, modern brick structure on the grounds today. Like its predecessors, the Ocean City Tabernacle continues to feature nationally prominent preachers of various denominations in the summer, drawing thousands of resort visitors to its services each year.

More than 100 years later, after its founding as a Christian resort, Ocean City is a city of churches. Whereas the first governing body on the island was the Ocean City Association, including a board of managers made up of three Methodist ministers, three Methodist laymen or ministers and three nonmembers or members of the Methodist Episcopal Church, today there is a fully secular City Council.

Nevertheless, the Christian Church has had a profound influence on the development of the community, a fact indicated by the large number of denominations represented in the city over the years.

# CHAPTER SEVEN

# *Those Ocean City Blues*

In keeping with its religious intent, the Christian resort established on Peck's Beach had from its start banned Sunday commerce. Ocean City's blue law, in one form or another, went on to become an integral part of life in the town.

In the *First Annual Report of the President of the Ocean City Association,* William B. Wood in 1880 explicitly laid out the denominational character basic to the town's founding: "Our great leading objects have been moral and religious — not secular.

"Let us not falter. A perfect Sabbath must be secured. Order and decorum must be maintained. The plumage of the white winged Angel of temperance must not be tarnished here!"

Wood's report, printed in 1881 by order of the association, distinguishes Sabbath rest and temperance as fundamental principles for the fledgling community.

"Being entirely separated from the main land, and surrounded by water, perfect control of the situation on the day of the Lord is assured," Wood promised. "Christian people will thus have exemption from various annoyances, and especially Sabbath desecration, characterizing fashionable watering places. It will be the aim of the managers to afford all residents within the precincts of their city by the sea as complete Sabbath rest as can well be enjoyed."

The third annual report lifts the wording about Sabbath rest almost straight out of the first, but the 1883 document also states that New Jersey laws provided "ample legal protection" for Sunday closings. However, in the fourth annual report, printed in 1885, the association recorded the beginning of resistance to its Sunday policy as originating in 1883.

> *"Let us not falter. A perfect Sabbath must be secured. Order and decorum must be maintained. The plumage of the white winged Angel of temperance must not be tarnished here!"*

In the report, Wood stated, "With the opening of the turnpike, and permission given for travel over the same to and fro to religious worship, some parties came to the conclusion that all our restrictions were abolished. This led to some thoughtless violations of our Sabbath restrictions, as to bathing and boating, early in the season. But as these cases were promptly attended to, such attempts at Sabbath desecration ceased, and our Sabbaths were peacefully and properly observed."

Wood's writing seems to take on a tone of moral righteousness as he continued: "It seems difficult to make some people understand our position, though we distinctly announced it at the first, and have reiterated it again and again.

"But we cannot allow mere pleasure or business transportation to or from Ocean City on the Lord's Day," he wrote. "Neither can we allow surf bathing, with all its concomitants of Sunday traffic and Sabbath desecration. When we conclude to give way to the clamor of a few persons who are not capable of rising to a moral altitude sufficient to enable them to see and understand our position, we must be consistent, and blot the name 'Christian' from our title."

From the time of Ocean City's incorporation in 1884, there had been disagreement about the effectiveness of city government in maintaining the Sunday restrictions previously enforced by the association. According to the fifth annual report of the Ocean City Association in 1885, "The borough authorities have not, in the estimation of some, been so prompt to enact ordinances guarding the Sabbath and restricting travel and pleasure-seeking on the Lord's day."

At the same time, the report noted with confidence, "The Christian sentiment of the place will be so strong that those administering the affairs of the borough will be influenced thereby to proper results, or others will be put in their places at the proper time, to maintain the character of Ocean City as a Christian Seaside Resort."

*The Sunday closing or "blue" laws were a tradition for supporters and a cause of frustration and amusement for opponents. Here, two summer visitors read a notice posted at a closed boardwalk shop on a Sunday in 1962.*

Wood, in the report, stated, "I have had the strongest personal assurances from the Mayor and some of the Councilmen of their sympathy with us in our moral and religious efforts."

Under the secular government, the wishes of the influential Protestant community finally were met with the passage on May 16, 1916 of Ordinance No. 80, titled "An Ordinance for the Suppression of Vice and Immorality in the City of Ocean City, New Jersey."

The first section of this initial blue law forbade concerts, shows, exhibitions, movies, vaudeville, opera, dance, entertainment, benefits, amusements, games and other pastimes on Sunday, whether they were paid or their sponsors accepted voluntary contributions.

The second section provided for a citation for persons allowing these activities to take place on their own or rented property, and the third part of the ordinance imposed a penalty of $200 or thirty days in jail for offenders. Religious services were exempted from the ban.

The simplicity of the early blue law was a far cry from the tangled legal confusion that would result in later years. The petitions of influential segments of the community and a desire to cooperate with modern trends led to the development of Sunday-closing ordinances so complicated that they became nearly impossible to maintain.

There was little question, though, when the city's first Sunday-closing law was passed in 1916, that it was the will of the people that the Christian Sabbath be kept closed to all commerce, and remain holy and quiet. Practically every kind of activity that might threaten this tranquility was outlawed, stiff penalties attesting to the seriousness of the matter.

However, just two years later, on June 24, 1918, a new ordinance was passed which, though specifying prohibitions against operating recreational facilities from pool halls to movie theaters, also granted permission for the sale of milk, newspapers, prepared foods and other items deemed worthy of exemption from the law.

The operation of toll bridges linking the island to the outside world, delivery of some perishables and of baggage, and the sale

*"Being entirely separated from the main land, and surrounded by water, perfect control of the situation on the day of the Lord is assured," Wood promised. "Christian people will thus have exemption from various annoyances, and especially Sabbath desecration, characterizing fashionable watering places. It will be the aim of the managers to afford all residents within the precincts of their city by the sea as complete Sabbath rest as can well be enjoyed."*

of goods "being of necessity" also were allowed under Ordinance No. 110. Ocean City's director of public safety was given the responsibility of determining what items were "of necessity," resulting in an arguably arbitrary system of selection by whoever occupied the post.

Still, the ordinance was a comprehensive one and reflected the wishes of the founders of the community to keep the city's Sunday a day set apart from the other six when the hustle and bustle characteristic of a resort town was given free rein.

In 1963, the tensions that had existed for many years between a large number of merchants and the religious community came to a head. In response to the wishes of the merchants, the Board of Commissioners, the municipality's governing body, decided to give the city's residents the opportunity to liberalize the ordinance that had stood for nearly half a century. Voters were asked to decide if they preferred to keep Ordinance No. 110 on the books or replace it with a less restrictive, if more arbitrary, law — Ordinance No. 947. There was no choice offered to abolish Sunday closings altogether, though, and arguments about the wisdom and fairness of that were to continue for decades.

On May 14 of that year, residents voted to endorse the more liberal of the two laws, and, even with a loosening of restrictions, three amendments would later be passed to allow an even greater amount of activity on Sunday.

In 1978, all "operations of Municipal, State and Federal governments" and "those recreational and cultural facilities … operated, sponsored or controlled by the City … not for profit and for which no fee other than a regulatory fee is charged" were permitted when voters endorsed Ordinance No. 1193. Two years later, a referendum put into law Ordinance No. 14-80, specifying that "nothing in this ordinance [947] shall be construed to prohibit works of necessity."

Finally, on September 11, 1986, in order to avoid litigation, City Council amended the blue law to exclude automatic bank tellers from the designation of prohibited commerce. The city's blue law solicitor had advised council that the machines' operation violated the Sunday-closing proscriptions. City officials subsequently ordered the machines closed on Sundays, but then turned around on their stance when a local bank filed a lawsuit against the municipality.

A further attempt to amend 947 by excluding coin-operated laundry machines and all types of food — unprepared or otherwise — was made about the same time but failed when

opponents to the blue law refused to support the amendment, calling it a softening of what was in any case an unjust law.

The amendments followed a year during which the island community was subject to no Sunday-closing law whatsoever. In 1985, a state appellate court ruled that blue laws were not in conformity with provisions of the state criminal code and therefore were superseded by it.

In June of 1986, however, the New Jersey Supreme Court overturned that ruling, automatically reinstating Ordinance 947. Suddenly, a community that had been getting used to open supermarkets and other conveniences available on the mainland was brought back to the restrictions that had been enforced, in one form or another, since the city's founding.

During the months that followed, some merchants and individuals who considered the blue law an anachronism began to resist the return of the old strictures. Some said blue laws are religiously motivated and discriminatory and therefore unconstitutional, although the U.S. Supreme Court had ruled against those contentions in the past.

Others called for an "all open" or "all closed" choice on the ballot to remove what they considered to be disparities in the ways in which the law affected different elements of the commercial community. Many also claimed they had suffered grave financial losses and were forced to discharge temporary employees because of the sudden reinstatement of the ordinance in the middle of the busy summer season.

In July, City Council agreed to place a binding referendum on the November ballot asking voters whether or not they wished to endorse an ordinance voiding Ordinance No. 947 and thereby removing Sunday-closing restrictions from municipal law. When the majority of voters answered, "Yes," in that referendum, it ended a tradition that, for better or worse, had been a part of Ocean City's history since its founding.

# CHAPTER EIGHT

# *Getting the Drop on Demon Rum*

On February 27, 1880, the Ocean City Association, in addition to outlawing "Sabbath desecration" and "all places of prostitution," "resolved that deeds of the Association shall forever prohibit the sale of all intoxicating liquors by whatever name they may be known."

Indeed, the *First Annual Report of the President of the Ocean City Association* is prefaced with a hymn entitled "Ocean City" in which the temperance theme is clearly pronounced:

> *This lovely isle, 'twixt sea and bay/ Unfettered still by demon's sway,/ For human rights we claim;/ That fearful curse, which heralds woe,/ Shall never here its shadow throw,/ We to the world proclaim./ Let freemen stand,/ On sea and land,/ And echo loud the same.*

A footnote at the bottom of the page specifically states that the"fearful curse" is "liquor traffic" which is "forever prohibited." Just in case the message still did not sink in, an entire paragraph in the report's description of the developing Christian resort is dedicated to establishing the association's position on alcohol:

"Intemperance is running riot through the land. By the sea, in the interior, everywhere, the black flag is floating in the breeze. The brewers, the distillers, the vendors, the guzzlers, claim their liberty — their liberty to drink and make drunk. How is this work of death to be arrested? Not by cowardly silence or conservatism, or do-nothingism. Agitation should be the watchword — agitation everywhere, persistent agitation. We must agitate until reason is re-enthroned, the public conscience purged, deep and pungent conviction of the enormity of this evil seizes upon the great heart of the Christian Church, and millions of stalwart

---

*"Intemperance is running riot through the land. By the sea, in the interior, everywhere, the black flag is floating in the breeze. The brewers, the distillers, the vendors, the guzzlers, claim their liberty — their liberty to drink and make drunk. How is this work of death to be arrested?"*

---

hands are ready to pull down the citadel of King Alcohol, leaving not one stone upon another. Ocean City will throw open its wide avenues and beautiful groves to the tramping feet of the temperance legions. We trust they will come, and setting the trumpet to the mouth, blow it so potently that the deep foundations of the kingdom of darkness will tremble, and a power go forth contributing to its utter downfall."

Among the religious activities listed in that first report is a National Temperance Convention scheduled for August 24 to August 28. There can be little doubt that the conventioneers found the welcome mat out in Ocean City. Three years and two annual reports later, a meeting of the National Temperance Society took place from July 7 to July 12. Speakers from Philadelphia, New York, and the Newark and New Jersey Conferences addressed the gatherings. The Lake brothers, the principal founders of the association and the city, had a tradition of temperance advocacy dating back to their grandfather. John Lake, a Quaker, was outspoken on the subject and also condemned the use of tobacco.

John's son, Simon, father of the Ocean City founders, must also have been vocal on the subject of temperance, because even after the deed restriction forbidding alcohol sales was in place, his sons continued to propagate the value of abstinence. Even the schools upon whose boards the Lake brothers sat were influenced by their prohibition stance.

The history of Ocean City's peculiar relationship with John Barleycorn predates its establishment as a city, though. In the centuries before the Lakes arrived on the island, it was a favorite party spot for mainlanders who would cross the bay to the isolated Peck's Beach, bringing along alcohol, food and musical instruments.

These activities and rumors that liquor was buried on the beach for use by revelers helped create a reputation for the place that led to its being nicknamed "Party Island." This image would change sharply with the founding of the association.

The isolationism of Ocean City's developers was accentuated by nearby Atlantic City's flaunting of immorality, with an estimated 14.55 saloons per 1,000 population, gambling houses, opium dens and brothels. At one point, the governor of New Jersey threatened to deploy military forces to the city to enforce state laws against open bars on Sunday.

Meanwhile, although local and visiting pastors to Cape May County communities advocated prohibition, merchants throughout the county were resistant. Yet of the six counties in South Jersey, only Cape May favored alcohol sales and consumption, concerned that legally enforced temperance would destroy the tourist trade. And, when the 18th Amendment, prohibiting the sale and use of alcohol, was proposed, New Jersey was the last state to ratify it. Nevertheless, when Prohibition became the law of the land, ministers on the island were quick to point out that on this issue Ocean City had been ahead of its time.

The 1986 anti-blue law battle resurrected fears that the alliance of people seeking to dismantle Sunday closing laws also would seek the legalization of alcohol sales. Although the ban on liquor continues to this day, the question, concern and debate resurfaces regularly.

# CHAPTER NINE

# Flirty Flappers and Beach Tarzans

It is said that hemlines rise and fall with the health of the economy. That may or may not hold true, but moral custom certainly has held greater sway over what is appropriate dress for the beach.

In the 1700s and 1800s, the sexes were separated for sun and surf bathing. The men, protected by the thick foliage and trees on South Jersey's barrier islands, swam entirely in the nude. The women, however, wore long, dress-like, woolen or flannel suits. Sometimes just old clothing sufficed.

Chastity was not the only reason women dressed so completely for the beach. Tanning was considered unattractive and unhealthful in those days; only those whose class required them to work outdoors were likely to get a tan, and wide-brimmed hats, parasols and skin-lightening lotions were used to keep a fair complexion.

The attire selected was no encumbrance to female beachgoers, as people rarely really swam in the ocean but merely waded in waist-deep and dunked themselves. Even so modestly dressed, women bathed privately and would only reunite with the men after they had returned to the bayberry and cedar trees for their dry street clothes.

One influence of the sea and beach has held true throughout time, however. Following a session in the salt water, bathers found the beach a romantic site for flirtation and courting. A sure sign of a woman's popularity among the opposite sex was the number of males who requested permission to dry her hair. Men would cut in as though on a dance floor.

*These fashionable beachgoers of the 1920s might seem overdressed today, and their dog would not be permitted on the beach. The raised bathing suits raised eyebrows as fashions changed (facing page), but the parasol reflects the healthful style of avoiding the sun's direct rays.*

Although segregation by gender ended sometime in the 19th century, the moral imperative for modesty continued well into the 1900s. At the turn of the century, suits were a bit more revealing but also more uniform in style: blue flannel trimmed in white. By 1907, bloomers became the rage, and with the fashion came a greater need for suitable stockings to cover the legs of the wearers.

It was only a matter of time before the more adventurous began rolling down or taking off their stockings, and some resorts felt it their duty to assign policemen the job of patrolling the beaches to enforce some semblance of decency.

Tape measure in hand, each of these happy warriors would comb the sands measuring the difference between stocking and bloomer lengths. Following a great deal of humiliation over the issue, in the 1920s a visitor from Los Angeles belted one of these officers in Atlantic City, breaking his glasses. Louise Rosine was taken directly to jail, from which she issued a statement asserting her right to bare her knees at the beach. In 1924, stockingless legs for women were declared legal in Atlantic City.

Another legal imposition on women was a law which said that, even in the full-dress regalia required for women when bathing, they nevertheless must wear a mackintosh (trenchcoat) over their suits while walking to and from the beach. By the 1930s, laws of this type had been repealed.

As for men, once the sexes were permitted to intermingle on

*Miss New Jersey 1925, Jeanette Darby Stokes, poses on the Ocean City beach. A young bather is cited for violating a city ordinance on proper attire by policewoman Lillian Olney (facing page). "This is a family resort!" she seems to be saying, as Mayor Harry Headley stands by.*

the beach, shirts as well as trunks were required. A gradual refusal by men to comply with this regulation resulted in increasing numbers of arrests of these "semi-nude bathers," and newspapers which supported their cause threw their editorial weight behind the men they referred to as "Tarzans of the Beach." In 1941, Atlantic City legalized this "topless bathing," but laws against it stayed in effect in Ocean City until years later. Still, into the 1960s it was against the law for men to appear topless anywhere but the beach.

In any case, from Ocean City's earliest days, bathing on Sunday was proscribed. In 1882, this prohibition was openly challenged when George G. Lenning went for a dip in the ocean not only on Sunday but during church hours and made a bad example worse by thumbing his nose at the arresting officer. Believing the rule to be an infringement on his rights, Lenning refused to pay the fines levied against him and, questioning the authority of the Ocean City municipal court, filed an appeal in superior court in Tuckahoe. On August 12, 1882, that court upheld the Ocean City ruling.

Another ordinance was passed in 1885 punishing Sabbath bathing with a fine of $50 or ten days in jail. If sources are correct in identifying the previous punishment to have been a $1 fine and fifty cents in court costs, the city evidenced in its lawmaking a determination to end Sunday bathing once and for all.

Nevertheless, in 1887, the Sunday beach-closing ordinance was repealed over the veto of Mayor Gainer P. Moore, who voiced his support of the law in his dissent.

"I have conscientious scruples against lending my aid or influence to set aside any law or ordinance based upon or working in unison with the higher or moral code, written by the fingers of the Almighty," Moore stated.

Since Moore's day, attitudes and customs have changed to accommodate a more pluralistic society in Ocean City, but, though no longer legislated, quiet Sundays remain a treasured tradition.

# CHAPTER TEN

# *Saving Lives Through the Years*

It's difficult to pinpoint just when the history of the Ocean City Beach Patrol begins. Federal lifesaving stations were created in 1871. Before the founding of the city and by the end of the century there were at least four such stations on the island. However, these units are more accurately identified as precursors of Coast Guard stations, reporting and aiding shipwreck victims.

As early as 1890, uniformed lifeguards appeared in photographs, but the Ocean City Beach Patrol was officially founded in 1920. Captain Jack Jernee is said to have started the patrol, and he ran his outfit in military fashion: with a great deal of discipline. His lieutenant, Tom Williams, took over the position in 1942. Under Williams' tenure, the OCBP entered an era of competition with other lifeguard units in which Ocean City tallied a number of important victories. In 1949, the patrol won the South Jersey Championships and for the following twenty five years the Ocean City squad either won the title or shared it.

Among the many men who served the beach patrol, a few names come to the fore immediately. The late T. John Carey and John B. Kelly Jr. are among them. Carey and Kelly were friends, patrol buddies, and each in his own way is a part of the mythology of Ocean City.

"Kell," as his friends and family called him, was raised to be a rower. His father, John B. Kelly Sr., was a Philadelphia contractor with a love of competition who taught his son to row at age five. The elder man had won two gold medals in Olympic rowing races and wanted his son to know the satisfaction of pitting his strength and endurance against competitors.

The patriarch had donated perpetual trophies to Ocean City's beach patrol for its annual races and was proud when his son won the competitions on two occasions. "Kell" was an inspiration to other young men on the patrol, according to those who served with him, and never lost his love of boating.

Carey was a favorite of Kell's father, and T. John's wife, Elizabeth, recalls that John B. presented him with his first surfboard. He returned the favor by teaching the Kelly children — including the girl who would grow up to be Princess Grace of Monaco — how to surf.

A proficient athlete, T. John also was a winner of the John B. Kelly Perpetual Award. Besides leaving his mark on the beach patrol, Carey's memory is kept alive in the many hand-crafted plaques he made for notable individuals and groups in and beyond Ocean City. To have been "plaqued" by Carey was a distinction worthy of note, and many public buildings display the awards.

Apart from its celebrities, though, the Ocean City Beach Patrol is unique in its sense of tradition and fraternity. Guards who served decades ago remain friends and colleagues, their favorite memories associated with their time on the patrol.

Jim "Butch" Macallister and Bill Ashmead, both of Philadelphia, are two such long-time friends who guarded together in Ocean City in their younger days. At age sixty, when he shared his story,

*Mayor Harry Headley presents the National Rowing trophy to Ocean City lifeguards Bob Stretch and Bert Loper in 1934. T. John Carey is at the rear, center.*

Jim had spent sixty one summer seasons in Ocean City.

"I was born September 9th and my mother carried me down here for the summer before I was born," Macallister said, "and I never missed a one."

At sixteen, Macallister passed the test to become a lifeguard and from 1943 through 1950 served on the beach patrol. He was a member of a rowing team that was awarded the John B. Kelly Perpetual Trophy, given to teams that won the Ocean City lifeguard races three years in a row.

The '40s were a great time to be a lifeguard in Ocean City. The Anchorage Hotel in Somers Point was a favorite watering hole. Here beers were a dollar a dozen. Dancing also was an evening diversion for members of the patrol.

"There was a place up on the boardwalk where we'd go dancing," Ashmead said. "The place was called Matt's. It was at First Street and the boardwalk, and a Mr. and Mrs. Matthews owned it. It had a jukebox, five songs for a quarter and everybody danced on the boardwalk. They had hundreds of kids there. That was the time of Artie Shaw and his Gramercy Five and Harry James and Benny Goodman — the big band era."

Also about that time, Convention Hall (the old Music Pavilion) sponsored dances. Hundreds of young people filled the historic building for the events. "If there were a thousand kids in there dancing, it wouldn't be crowded," Macallister said. "That became the Mecca after Matt's."

The boardwalk lights at that time were painted black with one small square of dark blue because of blackout rules during World War II when German submarines were very near to shore. "It was practically like walking down the boardwalk at midnight," Macallister recalled. "You could hardly see anybody. Anyway we would all meet down at Matt's. It was a

wonderful time to be down here. Of course it's still a wonderful time for a kid to be down here, but we sure had a ball."

Before going dancing, the lifeguards would meet at the Chatterbox Restaurant at Ninth Street and Central Avenue. "This would be from about six o'clock in the evening and the gals used to sit in the booths, and the guys would look in the windows and see who they might want to talk to," Macallister said.

"If they had a quarter they might buy them a Coke," he continued. "I was rowing and didn't get through until about eight o'clock each night, so I went down there for dinner, and I remember a Number Four, which was a ham and Swiss cheese combination club sandwich, lettuce and tomato. That was forty five cents, and the Number One was lettuce, tomato and egg salad, I think, and that was about thirty cents. And a steak dinner I think was ninety five cents. The good old days. Of course, nobody had any money anyway, so what difference did it make?"

The lifeguard's pay scale was one difficult obstacle to overcome. "We weren't paid an awful lot of money on the lifeguards," Ashmead said. "In those days, when we joined the life-

guards, the pay was $90 a month. All your uniforms were taken out of your pay; you paid for your uniform except for the whistle. If it rained, and you didn't work, you didn't get paid.

"Jim Macallister can remember that after the taxes were taken out, we got paid $45 every two weeks. After uniforms, taxes and rainy days, I think he cashed a paycheck for $17 one time. So you

Ocean City Life Guards, Ocean City, N. J.

*Ocean City lifeguards apparently wore homemade uniforms in 1890, but obviously with pride. Facing page: The men of the United States Lifesaving Service stand with Captain Mackay Corson (center) saved shipwreck victims from their station in Ocean City.*

*In this 1944 group photo of the Ocean City Beach Patrol, well-known as a member Jack "Kell" Kelly is pictured second row from the top, fifth from the right.*

had to have either a place to live or someone to help you because it was so difficult.

"Then the pay scale went up to a fantastic $100 for the second year and $105 for the third. And after the war, in 1946, we finally, through the threat of a strike, got the pay up to $120 for people who had three or four or five years or more."

Empty pockets notwithstanding, Ashmead said, "We were very fortunate we were the right age, doing the right thing, which was lifeguarding, at the right time, which was after World War II. Those first four years from 1946 to 1950 were fantastic years. We made an awful lot of friends whom we've still kept in touch with over forty years."

*A lifeguard race in the early 1930s.*

# CHAPTER ELEVEN

# The Kelly Clan

To gauge how Ocean City people feel about the well-known Kelly clan, open a conversation about them. Talking to anyone who knew them when the entire family spent its summers here, you'll soon discover a softening in the tone of voice, a kind of reverence in the way the person describes them. To island dwellers, seasonal or year-round, the Kellys were the Camelot Kennedys of Ocean City, as if the royalty Grace assumed by marriage was just an endorsement of what everyone knew all along.

John B. Kelly Sr. and his wife, Margaret Majer Kelly, owned a home on Henry Avenue in Philadelphia but spent their summers in their beachfront house at 26th Street and Wesley Avenue. Their children, Margaret, John B. Jr., Grace and Lizanne, spent some of their happiest times at their home "down the shore" in Ocean City.

As a young man, John B. had been an athlete, and a competitive one. A story familiar to most Ocean City residents is that of Kelly's self-discipline and training to reach his goal of winning the Diamond Sculls rowing competition at Henley-on-Thames in England. When he was ruled ineligible because he worked with his hands, he went on to win gold medals in the Olympics, two in 1920 and another in 1924. His daughter Margaret "Peggy" Kelly Conlan recalls the events.

"In those days, if you worked with your hands, if you were a laborer of any type, you were not permitted to row in the Henley, because it was for gentlemen, and they felt it gave him an extra advantage

being a working man, so my father could never row in the Henley regatta," she said. "Then in the Olympics, my father won the singles and doubles in 1920 and in '24 he won the doubles. He beat the winner of the Diamond Sculls in the Olympics, so it didn't matter too much to him, but he was a little annoyed and hurt that he could not row in that, but then they changed the rule and my brother was able to row in it and he won it twice."

John B. Sr. supported the Ocean City Beach Patrol by donating trophies to it for annual competitions but also by befriending some of the guards. As their beach house was somewhat removed from more developed areas, it would have fronted an unprotected beach were it not for the rapport between the elder Kelly and the patrol. One lifeguard who remembers serving at the home site was William Ashmead.

"One year I had the distinction of working for about three weeks in the early part of the season at 26th Street," Ashmead recalled. "They were very nice. The Kelly family was great to the lifeguards. Grace, who later became Princess Grace of Monaco, would bring us down sandwiches and milk and sodas and anything else we wanted. Grace was probably about 16 at the time. At that time, who knew that she'd become that famous?"

Peggy Conlan remembers the relationship between her family and the guards as well, saying that she and her sisters, once they were of "dating age," used to see them socially and that her brother and father were very involved with the beach patrol.

"My brother was always the mascot, so we always knew the lifeguards," she said. "There were very few people on our beach in the early days; in fact, we used to think that we lived in the sticks, but of course there was never any building like there is today. My father was always with the lifeguards and he used to take rows with them early in the morning or after they were off duty."

For his part, John B. Jr., informally known as "Kell," also loved to row. Some of his colleagues from beach patrol days remember

*Grace Kelly, about age 17 (right) and Lizanne with their father at the family's summer home at 26th Street and Wesley Avenue. Facing page, clockwise from left: Grace, Margaret Majer Kelly, Jack, Peggy, John B. Sr., and Lizanne.*

his foregoing some of the guards' socializing in order to keep to his rigorous training routine.

"Kell loved to row," Ashmead said. "Even in his later days when he was in his 50s, he would row against his son. He was a tremendous competitor."

Tragically, on the day he died of a heart attack — March

2, 1985 — Kell was jogging to the Philadelphia Athletic Club on Broad Street in Philadelphia after a period of rowing on the Schuylkill River near the famous Boat House Row. According to Peggy, this was not an unusual exercise for the athletic Kell.

When most people think about the Kellys, though, they think of Grace. A beautiful movie actress, then princess, Grace Kelly lived to a young maturity to be honored by the pope, who named her to lead an international council on family life. Ocean City folks remember her with a mixture of familiarity and devotion.

*Jack and Grace stroll the Ocean City beach with their father, John B. Kelly Sr., above. In September 1954 screen star Grace was photographed on the beach, right, while visiting the family home when she was serving as a judge in that year's Miss America Pageant.*

Perhaps her greatest fan on the island is Kate Field, whose collection of Princess Grace photographs and memorabilia is extensive. A neighbor and friend of the Kellys in Ocean City, Field remembers the visits of the married and crowned Princess Grace and the hubbub her youngest daughter, Stephanie, raised at the Ocean City beach house.

"Stephanie has always been a high-spirited girl," Field explained.

"One time in particular I remember I was over there at the mother's house and there were so many people around. Stephanie was about eight or nine and she had this skateboard, and she rode it up and down the terra-cotta hall, and I thought it would drive everybody crazy. Then, all of a sudden, she made this gigantic leap up onto this structure that was in the corner, and her grandmother finally said, 'Put that skateboard away.' I didn't think of them as royalty; they had such a great sense of humor."

Peggy often reminisces about the days when she and her siblings

*Prince Rainier of Monaco and Princess Grace visit the Kelly family home in Ocean City.*

were the children in the 26th Street house. Most of her thoughts are of "having just a great, great time," but there was work to be done, too.

"Our school didn't start too early; after Labor Day, you know we went to a convent school," she said. "When all of our friends went back to school, we stayed down for another two weeks or so. A Mr. Cohen had a wonderful fruit stand at 14th and Asbury Avenue, and Mother had dealt with him for years. So, when we saw those baskets of peaches and tomatoes on the back porch, we knew we had to get to work.

"He wanted to get rid of them after Labor Day, and my mother, being German, was very, very handy around the kitchen," she continued, "and we had to peel and put up in mason jars all the fruit and everything. So the three of us — Grace, Lizanne and Peg — all had to do the peaches and the fruit. Ah, did we all hate it. But we did it; we all pitched in."

Carol Macallister, who as a young girl worked at the Chatterbox Restaurant at Ninth and Central Avenue, knew Grace at the private Stevens School the two attended in Philadelphia. Also, since the youngsters lived just five houses apart on Henry Avenue, they knew each other quite well.

"Grace was a very pretty girl," Macallister said, "and she was a beautiful runner, if you can be a beautiful runner. She was a graceful person and a beautiful dancer. I could never understand why Hollywood didn't play up her dancing."

The genuine affection Grace inspired was a reason for the shock experienced by the entire town of Ocean City when she died on September 14, 1982 following an automobile accident. Kate Field recounted the effect the news had on her:

"I'll never forget hearing it because I was taking laundry down and I went to reach for a clothespin and I couldn't touch it," she said. "That's how paralyzed I was. I went to Lizanne's [Grace's sister], and by the time I got over there Lizanne was on the phone and I wrapped my arms around her and said, 'My God, I can't believe what we're hearing.' All Lizanne kept saying was, 'Isn't it terrible; isn't it terrible?'

"The phone rang," she said, "and then they got the official word. I don't think it was five minutes … we looked out the picture window on the sand dunes … there were cameramen out there. And Don [Lizanne's husband] said, 'How can they do this to us now?'"

Another summer resident, Grace's cousin, former Secretary of the Navy John Lehman, eulogized her in a casual statement during a visit to Ocean City in 1987: "Grace was one of the most impressive and beautiful human beings I have ever known."

Just three years after Grace died, her brother Kell suffered his fatal heart attack within hours of the death of their sister Peggy's husband, Gene.

"My brother and my husband died the same day," Peggy said. "It was a strange thing. They both fell dead in town (Philadelphia], a couple of blocks from each other, several hours apart, and of exactly the same thing."

Each summer, members of the Kelly clan return to their Ocean City home, and the Kellys and their cousins, the Lehmans, look forward to the family's annual athletic and bake-off competitions at the Lehmans' 46th Street house.

"The families are so big, actually," Peggy said, "the children and grandchildren and all. There's body surfing, and it ends with a tug of war, and there are all kinds of events. We have different judges every year. One year it was Grace, and T. John Carey was always one of the judges. Then we have a big chicken bake-off.

"We have different judges every year for the big bake-off," she continued. "One year, my brother Jack got Frank Purdue as one of the judges. Frank came for the weekend."

*"The Kelly family was great to the lifeguards. Grace, who later became Princess Grace of Monaco, would bring us down sandwiches and milk and sodas and anything else we wanted. Grace was probably about 16 at the time. At that time, who knew that she'd become that famous?"*

The Kellys have always lent an element of class to Ocean City, whether it be of the Olympic, the Hollywood or the royal kind. Along with the Lakes, they have left an indelible stamp on the character of the community.

"I think the Kellys were role models," Field said. "I think they meant stability. There were many times in their lives when they met with difficulties, and they showed that you just have to hang in there and pull together to make it through."

# CHAPTER TWELVE

# Generations of the Ocean City Boards

*At Park Place and the Boardwalk a person could buy an ice cream cone and sit under the roof of a shady pavilion.*

Like the seaside resort itself, Ocean City's boardwalk maintains a unique character that distinguishes it from similar promenades at the Jersey shore. Strolling the boards in the evening is a custom as traditional as sunning and swimming at the beach in the daytime.

The atmosphere of the broad walkway has the carnival sounds and smells to be found at Wildwood or Atlantic City, but the visual tone is less gaudy, and the people leisurely walking the Ocean City boards seem more relaxed and less frantic somehow. The city's motto of "America's Greatest Family Resort" is taken seriously by residents and merchants who guard the tone of the town. Also, the family orientation of visitors attracted to the resort creates a demand for the homey, old-fashioned-style promenade identified with an earlier era.

A slice of Americana on the Ocean City boardwalk, above. Facing page: The view from the Flanders Hotel porch in the mid-1920s; the Hippodrome Pier is at right.

Today's boardwalk is the latest in a line dating back to the late 19th century. In fact, one of the first thoroughfares in town was a boardwalk of sorts, built in 1880. In the *First Annual Report of the President of the Ocean City Association,* the Rev. William B. Wood describes the laying of "1,000 feet of board walk from the wharf on Fourth street to West avenue."

That first, ground-level boardwalk was primarily built as part of a roadway project to facilitate transportation from the landing on the bay to Parker Miller's house at around Seventh Street and Asbury Avenue. Miller was the main provider of hospitality on the island at the time.

Wesley, Ocean, West and Asbury avenues all were created then to afford access to important locations on the island. The final product, according to Wood, was "a continuous walk from the

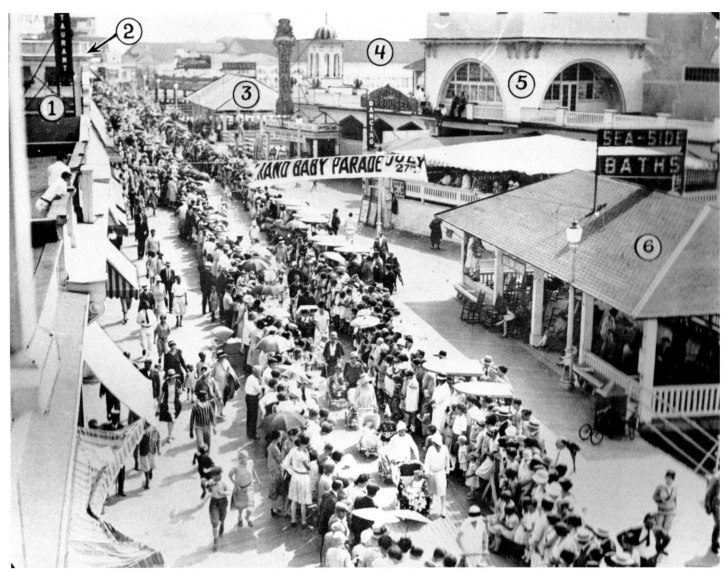

The Baby Parade of 1927 moved along a section of boardwalk that would be devastated by fire on October 11 of that year. Facing page: the aftermath of that fire; the Flanders Hotel is in the distance. In the Philadelphia Evening Bulletin photograph, above, the numbers indicate businesses that were destroyed in the fire.

wharf to the Ocean and around two sides of the Camp Grounds and Parks."

Some type of boardwalk is reported to have been built in 1883. Accounts are vague as to its exact location, but it seems that it extended from around Fourth Street to Seventh Street. In 1887 it was continued to 11th Street but in the following year was destroyed by a winter storm that wiped out many island structures. Ocean City built a bigger, better boardwalk after that catastrophe, and by 1898 it ran as far south as 13th Street.

Incidentally, a little-known boardwalk was built in the south end in 1908 and extended from at least 56th to 58th streets.

As most Ocean City history has focused on the area radiating from the Tabernacle grounds, between Fifth and Sixth streets and Wesley and Asbury avenues, little is known about the south end walkway and its ultimate disposition.

By 1904, two downtown boardwalks stood parallel with each other between Seventh and Ninth streets. Ironically, this situation developed because of land title disputes arising from a growing beachfront — a problem many citizens would be happy to face in this latter part of the century.

The two-block-long outer boardwalk was joined to the older inner boardwalk by an Eighth Street pier and a narrow Ninth

*A view from 58th Street of a little-known boardwalk build in the south end around 1908; the walkway ended at 56th Street.*

Street connection. A second outer walk was built between 10th and 11th streets and, for at least one summer, stood like a lone crane on its pilings in the water, inaccessible from the beach or the old boardwalk.

Once the deed rights issues were resolved, the outer boardwalk, about one-half block oceanward of the older boardwalk, was completed and the older one torn down. The wooden walkway that remained developed into a romantic thoroughfare boasting the best of Americana. Photographs of the boardwalk during its first three decades show breezy strollers — the men often wearing straw hats, the women carrying parasols — moving past ice cream parlors, vaudeville theaters and the ever-present salt water taffy confectionaries.

The boardwalk was to stand until 1927, when the worst fire in Ocean City's history swallowed it up in its fury. On October 11 of that year, the fire began in a pile of trash under the boardwalk at Ninth Street. Surging, southeasterly winds flung flames left and right of the point of ignition, spreading destruction to most of the boardwalk and to Ninth Street and 10th Street properties as far west as Wesley Avenue.

Firefighters from Somers Point, Sea Isle City, Tuckahoe, Northfield, Linwood, Pleasantville, Margate and Atlantic City joined their Ocean City colleagues in a desperate attempt to halt the onslaught of the wind-whipped blaze.

One eyewitness of those events remembered the appearance of a burning Ninth Street pier as giving the impression that the ocean itself was ablaze. When the Normandie Hotel became engulfed in fire, the flames reached hundreds of feet in the air, making the inferno visible for twenty five miles.

Nor was the impact of the tragedy contained by the waters surrounding the island. Cinders capable of igniting new fires were carried across the bay to Somers Point, where residents were careful to douse them as they landed.

Also, one shameful note of mainland history was disclosed by an Ocean City observer of the fire. It seems that many people whose properties were in the line of destruction removed to the beach what few belongings they could retrieve before their buildings ignited. According to one eyewitness, looters from the mainland exploited the opportunity to pillage many of these last surviving personal effects while the fire victims were being relocated.

Characteristic of its predecessors, a new boardwalk rose like a phoenix from the ashes of the old, and this last structure, in the main, is the one still standing today. By July 4, 1928 enough of the restoration had taken place — from Sixth to 12th Street — that the first section was dedicated by Mayor Joseph G. Champion.

Champion drove a golden spike through a bronze plaque commemorating the event on the boardwalk in front of the new Music Pier at Moorlyn Terrace, although that building would not be completed until the following year. The plaque is now enshrined at the Ocean City Historical Museum.

At the next year's Fourth of July ceremony, the completed boardwalk, which ran from Second to 12th streets, and the Music Pier were celebrated.

Built with fir from Washington state and redwood from California, the boardwalk was anchored by reinforced concrete pilings, driven into the sand by hydraulic pressure. The 32-foot-long, 18-inch-square piles weighed more than five tons each and concrete beams and girders reinforced the walk.

City Engineer William H. Collison Jr. and his brother and assistant, N. Harvey Collison, who designed the boardwalk were innovators, as the stable structure was the first of its kind at the time.

In contrast, the first boardwalk in the country was collapsible, and was brought out and taken up each season in neighboring Atlantic City. Not only did it have no stable moorings but it lacked railings, and, according to some reports, pedestrians frequently fell off the walk.

---

*One eyewitness of those events remembered the appearance of a burning Ninth Street pier as giving the impression that the ocean itself was ablaze. When the Normandie Hotel became engulfed in fire, the flames reached hundreds of feet in the air, making the inferno visible for twenty five miles.*

---

The original Ocean City boardwalk, built in 1883, was of a more permanent variety, but it and its replacements following natural catastrophes were not as sturdy as the Collison creation.

Even with its concrete substructure, though, the 1929 boardwalk was affected by the forces of nature. By 1935, the wooden beams of the promenade were seen to be rotting and continual replacement has been a part of the maintenance of the boardwalk ever since.

When the boardwalk was in the planning stages, it was decided to move it yet another half-block closer to the water's edge, a move that proved deleterious to a beach that, unknown to the engineers of the time, had begun to erode. Their intention was simply to move the boardwalk and its businesses closer to bathers on the wide strand.

By 1986, the recession of the sands around Seventh and Ninth streets had become so pronounced that engineering studies of possible ways to save the once broad beach were ordered by the city administration. Replenishing and keeping sand on the downtown, boardwalk-fronted beaches have become one of the greatest challenges to the city in the latter part of this century.

While the beaches have been susceptible to storms, the boardwalk itself has endured periodic bashings. The worst of these occurred on September 21, 1944. A hurricane moving north at a rate of about 35 mph but packing winds of up to 74 mph and gusts of 91 mph struck Ocean City, starting early in the afternoon with a gentle rain. By about 4:30 p.m., traffic was halted, and by 6 p.m., most of the island was submerged.

The worst damage to the boardwalk occurred north of Sixth Street, and dunes north of First Street were washed away by the surf. According to an account by the state Department of Environmental Protection, although the amusement pier at Plymouth Place was devastated, a Ferris wheel on that pier (Gillian's Fun Deck) remained unharmed. Another account states that curiosity seekers rode the amusement the next few days to get a bird's-eye view of the damage.

In 1960, Hurricane Donna, though 80 miles out to sea, caused a great deal of damage by thrusting fierce ocean waves against the boardwalk. Ironically, according to the DEP, the boardwalk had just been re-decked at a substantial cost to the city.

A northeaster in 1962 destroyed or badly damaged the boardwalk north of Fourth Street and south of 12th Street. Boardwalk decking between 12th and 23rd streets was torn from its pilings and carried toward Central Avenue, according to the DEP's Bureau of Flood Plain Management. Also, two fishing piers, at 14th Street and 59th Street, and the beach patrol headquarters at 10th Street were almost completely destroyed.

About the last significant blow to the boardwalk was the loss of the old Convention Hall, previously called the Music Pavilion, in 1965. A March blaze at Sixth and the boardwalk ended the history of the landmark building, which was the predecessor of the Moorlyn Terrace Music Pier.

The amusement piers, souvenir and gift shops, and restaurants and food vendors on the boardwalk add to the flavor of Ocean City summers as much as the wooden walkway itself and the Music Pier situated on it.

Many of the oldest, most traditional shops still stand. Steel's Fudge and Shriver's candy store continue to offer their confections alongside newer shops that offer their wares to the thousands of people who stroll the Ocean City boardwalk on pleasant summer evenings.

## CHAPTER THIRTEEN

# *A Pier Without Peer*

The Ocean City Music Pier is the seaside resort's most famous and beloved landmark. The arches and gingerbread of the stately building have made it a favorite subject and background for photographers, amateur and professional.

Moreover, along with the Flanders Hotel, the Pier is an architectural welcome mat, greeting returning summer visitors to the island. As the John Wanamaker eagle acts as a landmark for Philadelphians, the Music Pier serves as an identifiable meeting spot for people on the boardwalk.

*The "New Convention Hall," the Music Pier, was built between 1928 and 1929 at Moorlyn Terrace and the Boardwalk.*

However, the present structure is only the latest of a number of music houses run by the city, its immediate predecessor being the Convention Hall which stood at Sixth Street and the Boardwalk. That white frame building earlier had been called the Music Pavilion, and its first site, oddly enough, had been Moorlyn Terrace and the Boardwalk, a stone's throw from where today's Music Pier now stands.

The Pavilion was moved to Sixth Street following the 1927

*The original Music Pavilion at 8th Street and the Boardwalk, above, was moved in 1928 to 6th Street, after the previous year's boardwalk fire. The interior of the Music Pavilion, below.*

fire that destroyed the boardwalk, which at that time stood about half a block west of the present structure. The devastating blaze resulted in the city's decision to construct a new wooden way closer to the ocean on what was then a much broader beach.

The reconstruction plans would have placed the boardwalk between the ocean and the Pavilion, so the city commissioners chose to move the building to city-owned beachfront. At a cost of $40,000, the Music Pavilion was rolled along the beach to its Sixth Street location, where it was repaired and altered to make it functional as a convention center.

*Convention Hall — the original Music Pavilion — was destroyed by fire in 1965.*

At the same time that the Pavilion was moved and renovated, a new Music Pier, the Spanish-style structure now gracing the Ocean City beach, was built at Moorlyn Terrace. In June of 1928, construction began, and the Pier was finished by early the next year, at a total cost of $248,000.

The red tile roofing also covers the Chatterbox Restaurant and St. Augustine's Roman Catholic Church.

The Music Pier was one of many improvements, including the new boardwalk, which the city marked at its 50th anniversary celebration on July 4, 1929.

A 1965 fire leveled the Pier's predecessor, the Convention Hall, which at its Sixth Street locale had housed political rallies, beauty pageants, boat shows, boxing tournaments and concerts. From the 1940s to the 1960s, the center had presented city-sponsored record hops, spanning the musical eras from Glenn Miller to the Four Tops.

Before 1965, the Hall had been blessed, escaping fires and storms that had razed less lucky nearby structures. Only the Hurricane of 1944 had seriously damaged it.

However, after the 1965 blaze consumed the Hall, the Music Pier stood alone as the city's entertainment and ceremonial center. Lovers of all ages have strolled or sat on the benches of the Pier's

arched pavilion for sixty years, fittingly, as the approval for its construction was made on Valentine's Day, 1928.

Rising 20 feet above the sea at its easterly end, the, Pier stands firmly upon 111 concrete pilings, each two feet in diameter and 50 feet long. Its 60-by-85-foot dance floor has seen many a couple move according to the styles of the day before bands playing on its raised, big-band stage. The high-ceiling hall seats 1,100 people.

Though sturdy, the Music Pier has a compositional aspect that makes it vulnerable to the elements. The mortar of which it is made is porous and absorbs moisture. During the winter the building must be heated to keep it from sopping up water from air and sea.

In the early 1970s, the Arab oil embargo caused a cutback in fuel allocated for that purpose, and the result was the release of soggy clumps of ceiling in various parts of the building and water leaks as the cement became saturated.

The city fought back with gunite restoration of the pilings and coal tar epoxy treatment of the building itself, and regularly applied fresh coats of paint continue to keep the Music Pier as attractive as always.

*Crowds turn out to see a new boardwalk and Music Pier at dedication ceremonies July 4, 1929, top. At left: The Music Pavilion and Boardwalk in 1930.*

# CHAPTER FOURTEEN

# Sparring with Poseidon

*The Hurricane of 1944 caused extensive damage and brought extreme tidal flooding throughout Ocean City.*

If your single source of reference to the climate of Ocean City were the *Ocean City Guide Book and Directory,* published in 1895, you would give little thought to the explosiveness just below the surface of Nature's composed aspect, her mild sea breezes and sunny beaches.

"Nature has smiled in peculiar beneficence on the island upon which Ocean City is located," wrote Mary Townsend Rush in the directory. "It lies near the 39th degree of north latitude; on or near this parallel are the Azore Islands, noted for their equitable climate; the Balearic Islands of the Mediterranean Sea, Southern

*An aerial view of the storm-beseiged island during the March 1962 nor'easter shows four homes burning along Central Avenue at 41st Street. Facing page: tidal flooding during that storm at 4th Street from Atlantic Avenue to the boardwalk.*

frozen bays all have plagued Ocean City at various times.

Among the first recorded batterings taken by the early community was the so-called Mud Hen Storm in 1889. The hurricane hit New Jersey's barrier islands on Sunday, September 9, and dealt damage to several coastal towns, Ocean City among them, that were rebuilding following a serious blizzard of the previous year.

If the faith of those early Christian settlers was unshaken by that stormy season, the winter of 1889 certainly put them to the test.

Italy, with her vineyards and orange groves, bearing fruit in winter; the Ionian Isles, Arabia, the land of the date palm and tamarind; the central belt of the Flowery Kingdom, and the Yosemite Valley of California."

So "happy" is the location of the island that winter itself is tempered, and so "equable is the temperature the seasons seem to drift imperceptibly into one another," Rush observed.

As one might guess, the guidebook was written for distribution to visitors and potential tourists. Quite honestly, though, on a warm October afternoon, the island's climate is matchless, as anyone who has played truant to lie on the beach can attest.

Nevertheless, like the Roman god Janus, bearing a smiling countenance on one side of his head and a frowning one on the other, the elements play ruthless turnabout with the humans who inhabit the South Jersey barrier islands. Floods, hurricanes and

Some fifty years ago, Captain Lewis Risley described that bitter time to local historian Harold Lee, who included Risley's memories in his book *A History of Ocean City, New Jersey.* Risley noted that the Great Egg Harbor Bay was frozen solid, cutting off most supplies, which normally were ferried across the waterway from Somers Point. For about a month, the hardiest citizens made their way around town in horse-drawn sleighs, and, when even hay for the horses became scarce, a hotel owner made two sleigh trips across the bay and meadows to Marmora to bring the precious fodder into town.

The next serious natural calamity happened on August 20, 1933. Called a "dry northeaster," the storm, because of the relatively primitive weather forecasting of the day, caught a large number of boaters by surprise. About 100 vessels found themselves tossed by a tumult of waves that seemed to leap from the

calm seas without warning. Of the boaters unable to make it to shore, fifty were rescued and five drowned.

Former Ocean City lifeguards probably wouldn't characterize themselves as historians, but from their perch above the beach they have watched many of the outstanding events of the city's history, including its storms. Jim Macallister, a former lifeguard, described one meteorological happening of 1943 with the flair of an Edward R. Murrow.

"In 1943, I was assigned my first year on Ninth Street beach. And one of the memorable things of that year was this. One day I came to work and I walked down the boardwalk, and the waves were breaking from the horizon," he said. "Rolling all the way. There's never been such waves, even in a hurricane.

"It was so bad that the waves would come in like tidal waves and wash under the boardwalk," he said, "and they would go way out past the jetty on dry land. And it was extremely dangerous because if a kid would run down the boardwalk he'd be on dry land and suddenly there'd be six feet of wave coming at him. So we pulled everybody off the beach.

"Because of this freaky situation in which there were actually huge waves as far as you could see rolling in, we were able to take the mattresses, they called them floats, and for once in my life we could run out to dry land at the end of the jetty at Ninth Street and ride a wave in over dry land," he continued. "It'd just push us in on dry land. It was unbelievably rough. There must have been a small storm at sea."

Previous storms did little damage to the island itself when compared with the Hurricane of 1944. Producing 70-mph

*The March 1962 nor'easter stripped away entire sections of the boardwalk, above, moved homes off their foundations, and filled streets with beach sand and debris (facing page).*

*The Hurricane of 1944 devastated Ocean City's oceanfront, above and facing page.*

considered the highest elevation on the island — was under a foot and a half of water.

Naturally, the oceanfront and bayfront suffered some of the most severe damage; the boardwalk north of Second Street was completely gone and has never been replaced. The Music Pier and other boardwalk structures took a beating, and damages were estimated at $2 million.

City records list a cost of nearly $500,000 to repair facilities along the beach and bayfront. The toll taken in privately owned property was phenomenal, with at least fifty percent of the town's buildings experiencing some damage.

Utilities were hit hard as might well be expected. Gas, electric and telephone services were disrupted and some residents were without light or heat for more than a day. These services were not to return to normal for about a week.

According to a state Department of Environmental Protection report, in one incident a "four story home located at 4605 Central Avenue was turned into a two story structure when the first and second stories were removed by the storm and the third and fourth floors replaced them intact." Another DEP report states, "An observer noted that a dinner table floated by him, the table set with plates and dinnerware."

True or not, those stories reflect a general consensus that the storm seemed to have a mind of its own, ignoring potted flowers on one side of a street and totally destroying a house on the other.

Macallister also has vivid memories of the Hurricane of 1944. According to his recollection, the captain of the Ocean City

winds with gusts up to 91 mph, the hurricane created the highest surge ever recorded at Atlantic City's Steel Pier. Although it was traveling northward about 30 miles off shore, the storm slammed wind and rain into Ocean City that within an afternoon's time had covered practically the entire island with water.

Storm warnings alternated between hurricane and tropical storm alerts that September 14, so the city expected some type of trouble from the big wind. A gentle rain began to fall in early afternoon; by 4:30 p.m. the island was nearly closed off from the mainland; and at high tide, 6:36 p.m., the bay and ocean met. Even the City Hall area at Ninth Street and Asbury Avenue —

Beach Patrol put together a crew of lifeguards to get the boats off the beach.

"By about 2:00 p.m., the wind was blowing about 60 or 70 mph, and it was blowing so strong that it actually cut our legs," he said. "I remember that around Second Street we were pulling one boat up, and the sand had sandblasted the paint off the one side of the boat."

The former lifeguard remembers having taken part in the evacuation of the old beach patrol headquarters, affectionately called "the tent."

*The Ocean City Fishing Pier was torn apart by two construction barges that broke loose in a storm August 12, 1980.*

"After we cleaned the trophies out of the beach patrol headquarters, we were leaving it just as it was about to collapse, and the waves were breaking over the boardwalk and everything else," he said. "And Tenth Street was about five feet deep, I remember, and there was an old apartment building right in the back of the headquarters, where two old ladies were stuck on the top floor.

"And I remember this big guy, Bluto, went up and got both of them, and carried them, one on each arm, and kept their heads above water until they got back to about Wesley Avenue, where it was only about three feet deep," Macallister added. "But that was quite a storm, and it really raised a lot of Cain around O.C."

Unfortunately, the city's response to some of the damage caused by the storm was inadequate. Although reconstruction of city and privately owned structures followed fast on the heels of the storm, damaged bulkheads were left in disrepair. In fact, a working dune system that suffered some degradation from the hurricane was eventually bulldozed away in deference to building and parking lot construction.

November 25, 1950 was the day on which the next big storm hit Ocean City. A northeaster rather than a full-scale hurricane, it had winds measured at 72 mph. (A storm is deemed a hurricane when its winds reach 75 mph.) Water spilled over bulkheads along the beachfront and the bay, causing extensive damage from flooding. Electric and phone lines were downed by gale-force winds and water erosion exposed water and sewer lines.

Ten years later, a storm generated by Hurricane Donna struck on September 12. Though 80 miles out to sea at the time of its passing, wind gusts were reported at 80 to 84 mph at the U.S. Weather Bureau station at Pomona. Ocean waves damaged the newly re-decked boardwalk, and trees and antennas were torn down by the storm.

Those two storms had a minimal effect compared to the northeaster that assaulted the island from March 6-8, 1962. This storm, also known as the "Ash Wednesday Storm," created more damage than any other storm since the Hurricane of 1944. In addition, the beaches in 1962 were in a more vulnerable state than when they faced the blasts of September '44.

However, whereas the earlier storm hit the north end hardest, the '62 storm did its worst damage between 34th and 59th streets. About 800 buildings incurred some damage, over 600 needed major repairs, and 300 had to be razed.

At least six homes vanished completely. According to the Army Corps of Engineers, 6,587 structures were hurt, close to 2,000 of them structurally. Some houses simply floated off their foundations.

The bulkheads between 35th and 45th streets were destroyed by waves or washed out from beneath, and the piers at 14th Street and 59th Street were also wrecked, their debris acting as battering rams against other structures on the oceanfront.

Yet apart from the more dramatic elements of the storm, the inundation of the island by water did the most damage. Five successive high tides occurred concurrently with perigean spring tides, creating even greater flooding than the storm alone could muster. During peak tide on the last day of the storm the water was from two to three feet deep in the main streets of town.

Stores along Asbury Avenue suffered water damage.

The breakage of a gas main, which left some residents without service early in the storm, proved providential as many electrical fires ignited throughout town later. The earlier disruption and cutoff precluded an explosive situation which might have created more devastation and possibly loss of life.

About twenty four fires in all were caused by electrical shorts, and firemen found themselves foiled by water so deep that it was nearly impossible to get equipment close enough to the blazes to be effective. Three homes in the 3900 block of Central Avenue burned to the ground, along with a woodworking shop at 10th and West.

For two days, the island was cut off from the mainland, and shelters were set up at the Civil Defense Headquarters at 12th Street and Wesley Avenue, the Ocean City High School on Atlantic Avenue, and the Flanders at 11th and the Boardwalk. Emergency vehicles rushed to the south end to rescue stranded residents and take them to shelters; some of them were unable to return to their homes for two weeks while cleanup was taking place.

Part of the decking of the boardwalk between 12th Street and 23rd Street was torn from its pilings and landed near Central Avenue, and the portion that extended north from Second Street was washed out and never replaced.

Nearly six feet of sand was lost from the oceanfront beach, a harbinger of the severe erosion that would take place on a regular basis in the next two decades, prompting a cycle of pumping, erosion, and replenishment that now has become routine.

A recurrence of this beach battering happened on August 9, 1976, when Hurricane Belle passed Ocean City by, fifty miles out to sea. A hurricane warning was posted by the National Weather Service, and then the mayor called for an evacuation of the island, to which 60,000 people responded.

At around 3 p.m. that afternoon, police opened all four lanes of Ninth Street for outgoing traffic and the evacuation was carried out rather smoothly. By around 8:30 p.m., all entrances to the city were closed. Damages included about $450,000 in private and public property, including about $200,000 in beach erosion. The winds were reported at between 60 and 70 mph.

Just four years later, on October 24, 1980, two storms joined forces to create the fourth highest surge recorded at the Steel Pier. More than half the damage caused in Ocean City was beach erosion. An estimated 100 feet of beach were lost, as well as step ramps to the boardwalk.

On March 29, 1984, several barrier island communities found themselves virtually stranded as surging waves ripped into dunes, boardwalk and oceanfront houses.

Beach damage was estimated at $3 million, a loss of approximately one-half million cubic yards of sand, and the dredges and sandpumpers once again had a job to try to restore the ravaged beach. The second greatest material loss was automobiles. With salt water up to their headlights, cars in many parts of town were totally destroyed.

Besides the loss of privately owned automobiles, Ocean Pontiac at Eighth Street and West Avenue lost 150 cars and suffered an additional $1.5 million in damages to the showroom, offices and parts room.

Within a year, the sand had been replaced on the beach, shops were cleaned up and car owners, with or without sufficient insurance, had found new means of transportation. Then, in September of the following year, Gloria struck.

The powerful hurricane moved up the Atlantic seaboard in jerky patterns, blasted the South Jersey shore, and then traveled inland, where it hit the Philadelphia area with greater force than that with which it nipped Ocean City. Still, photographs of cars and trucks engine-deep in salt water testify to the serious damage the hurricane did do to property on the island. Ocean City reportedly lost about $1 million in sand where recent man-made methods of replenishment had been tried.

Like the legendary paradises of the South Seas, fertile, abundant in yield and cooled by sultry sea breezes, Ocean City and other New Jersey barrier islands are situated on a volcano of sorts — the constant threat of northerly moving tropical storms and fierce northeasters. Weather prediction constantly improves and residents now have the benefit of accurate forecasting and adequate preparation time to evacuate the island if need be.

Still, until someone devises the means not only to predict the weather but to control it, the island and all it holds will continue to be subject to the whims of Nature.

*Boardwalk and oceanfront damage after the Hurricane of 1944.*

# CHAPTER FIFTEEN

# The Elephants' Graveyard

Modern technology has enabled man to view the debris of vessels situated at the bottom of the deepest seas. Even the sunken *Titanic* had been first scrutinized by scientists and a curious public with the help of robots. Although the coastal waters off Ocean City hold no wrecked ships with that kind of notoriety, estimates are that at least a thousand ships lie close to shore here, covered either by water or sand.

In fact, sand often has been the culprit in these wrecks off the island's coast. The Great Egg Bar, which changes position and shape according to the whims of the sea, has snagged many ships which for various reasons have come within its grasp.

Some wrecks have become havens for sea life and magnets for sport fishermen. Others are attractions for divers, and a few have drifted into the realm of legend — most notably the *Sindia*.

Early records are hazy about the details of many of these maritime misfortunes, predictably so, since the island was not settled until the

*The British brig* Delight *foundered off Peck's Beach in 1779 and cannons were thrown overboard to lighten the ship. One was later recovered and stood on the grounds of the Tabernacle until the 1960s.*

end of the last century. Still, the mishaps that did occur have been noted, and though the records may be more heavily weighted with legend than with facts, the overall picture that emerges is consistent with the hazardous occupation of seamanship as it was practiced over the past few hundred years.

One of the earliest recorded shipwrecks in the area was that of the *Dolphin,* a Spanish galleon which sank near the Great Egg Bar in the 1600s. The stately vessel supposedly was heavily laden with gold and silver, and went down near Great Egg Harbor Inlet.

During the Revolutionary War, a number of British and American vessels foundered off the island's shore. The British brig *Delight* came aground in 1779 and was remarkable in that one of the cannons thrown overboard to lighten the ship was discovered twenty one years later and placed at the entrance to a road in Palermo, subsequently named Cannon Road. Finally, the piece was returned to the island and set on the grounds of the Tabernacle between Asbury and Wesley avenues, from which it disappeared in the late '60s.

When the ship first was stranded, local American militiamen boarded her and took her crew as prisoners of war to Philadelphia. The cargo was sold at public auction, but there were some serious inventory discrepancies between the time the *Delight* loaded aboard its shipment of rum and sugar in Jamaica, bound for New York, and when the merchandise was recounted following its forfeiture.

Sixty-six hogsheads of rum were unaccounted for. Rumor has it that the grog most likely was buried on the beach for later use at beach parties. Others speculate that the barrels found their way to taverns in South Jersey, Delaware and southeastern Pennsylvania, where a black market flourished.

An American ship named *Fame* also went down during the war.

*Local people were quick to answer calls for help from foundering ships. They often looted them too.*

The revolutionary government had dispatched the brig to protect Cape May County from a British invasion, and she had been successful in sinking several British ships.

But the *Fame* was destined to find her own final resting place in the Great Egg Harbor Bay, where she was capsized by strong winds on July 22, 1781. Though reports differ, it seems that about twenty men died and three to seven survived.

In December of 1815, a ship from France bound for New York got caught in a disastrous storm which pushed it shoreward, a calamity heightened by the captain's ill-fated decision to spread all sails in an attempt to make it to safety. Mainlanders worked the next morning to rescue survivors and though nine were saved, seven died.

The hull of that French ship, the *Perseverance*, remains offshore, still holding much of the $400,000 cargo. The rest, including silks, satins, china and glassware, was washed ashore on Ocean City beaches.

The 19th century brought a great wave of immigration to the United States, and two of the ships that foundered off the island carried hopeful Europeans intending to make America their home. In 1855, the brigantine *Cardiff*, carrying 300 German immigrants, ran aground off Peck's Beach, with but one casualty; and, in 1864, 250 Irish immigrants were saved from the sinking *Elizabeth*, which foundered on the Great Egg Bar.

Some of the sea disasters were acts of God, but others simply the result of human error. For example, the *Zetland* lost its captain to illness before the ship approached coastal New Jersey on its way to Philadelphia. Without a single crewman able to navigate the vessel, it beached at Ocean City on November 2, 1881.

This particular event was noted by William Lake in his diary: *"Zetland* Brigantine with cargo wrecked on the Beach northeast of Thirty-first Street. The crew of nine were rescued by the men of the Life Saving Station."

The creation of lifesaving stations, from which Coast Guard stations descended, actually may have been hastened by a local sea tragedy. In 1853, the *James C. Fisher,* en route from Smyrna Creek, Del., to New York City, was hit hard by headwinds as it approached the Great Egg Harbor Bay and sought a safe port to wait out the storm. On January 2 the ship went aground and one crewman decided to swim to shore for help.

Garrett L. Hynson made it ashore, found help, and went on to become a state representative. His publicized story, as well as his political efforts, provided impetus for the development of the U.S. Life Saving Service in 1871.

To form an idea of the large number of sunken vessels off the shore of Peck's Beach, consider this: *Heston's Annals*, published in 1904, surmised that a "submerged wreck," the S. *Thorn,* had held the *Sindia* in a vacuum grip — that the first ship was, in fact, beneath the second. Also, the document states that the wreck of a bark, the *Lawrence,* "was visible a short distance" from her, and that the hull of the brig *Perseverance* "was partially exposed at a place east by south" of the *Sindia*.

The reader of *Heston's Annals* certainly must have envisioned Ocean City as the elephant's graveyard of seaside towns.

# CHAPTER SIXTEEN

# *The* Sindia: *Our Sunken Treasure*

Quite literally, "it was a dark and stormy night" when the *Sindia*, thrown hard against the beach by furious winds, came to rest on a sandbar a mere 150 yards from Peck's Beach. The image of the stranded bark has become the single most familiar picture associated with Ocean City.

One report claims that the ship was named for an Indian royal family, Sindhia of the Mahratta dynasty, that ruled the central state of Gwahor of that subcontinent until a British conquest in 1844. Another suggests that she bore the name of Madagee Sindia, emperor of Hindustan, an East Indian state, from 1741

*The* Sindia, *a four-masted steel bark, depicted above, grounded on Peck's Beach December 15, 1901. It became a landmark and Ocean City's most famous shipwreck. Facing page: The* Sindia *shortly after it grounded that winter.*

to 1749. Whatever the true derivation of the name, the *Sindia* boasted a figurehead of a turbaned man on her bow, which indicated some connection with India.

The vessel was built in Belfast's Harland & Wolff shipyard in 1887 as, according to one source, a steamship. Then, in 1892, she was fitted with spars and canvas and converted into a bark with three square-rigged masts and a schooner-rigged mizzen mast.

The ship was 329.3 feet long and weighed 3,068 gross tons. She called Liverpool her home port and sailed about 200,000 miles in her journeys to and from India and the Orient.

Originally built for the Brocklebank shipping firm, she was sold to the Anglo-American Oil Co. for $200,000 in 1900. In

*A winter scene of the shipwreck, above. By 1940 shifting sands had covered the remains of the wreck of the* Sindia *and one of the ship's masts marked her grave (facing page). The ship's figurehead is now in the collection of the Ocean City Historical Museum.*

September of that year, she took on a cargo of oil bound for Shanghai, China.

She completed that mission and set sail for Kobe, Japan, where she was reloaded with camphor, silk, matting, oil, fine china, linseed, screens, wax and novelties. Also, legend claims that a large idol, possibly of the Buddha, was smuggled aboard, although this has never been proven.

On July 8, 1901, she set sail for New York City with her new cargo, whose estimated value ranged from $400,000 to $1.2 million. The trip was routine: across the Pacific Ocean, south to Cape Horn, then north, along the eastern coast of the Americas to the Empire City. All the way, it was smooth sailing. Then calamity hit.

Captain Allen McKenzie had brought the ship as far north as Cape May when a wintry storm slammed into the vessel. For four days, he was engaged in battle with the worst Poseidon could muster, and, on December 15, the winds first pulled the *Sindia* due west, then swung her around toward the south and shoved her toward the sands of Peck's Beach.

The wild wind and surf burrowed the hull of the craft ever deeper into the encompassing sand, and McKenzie signaled for help about 2:30 a.m. The sight of the signal flares and the cannon-like boom of the flapping sails caught the attention of Harry Young at the Ocean City lifesaving station and Edward Boyd at the Middle station on the mainland.

Each station dispatched a crew to the scene, the Ocean City station bringing a breeches buoy and Middle, a surf boat. Three failed attempts were made to shoot the breeches buoy to the ship in order to rescue the crew, and, at daybreak, the surf boat was launched.

The Ocean City station's Captain J. Mackey Corson and Middle's A. C. Townsend commanded the crew of about fifteen men. Howling winds and torrential rain hampered the boat's slow movement toward the ship, as Corson steered and called orders to the rowing crew.

Although McKenzie initially forbade his crew to leave the ship, he relented, and the rescue party transported the weary seamen in parties of seven to the beach, with the captain accompanying the last group. Thirty-three men were saved that day by the speedy action of the rescue stations.

Rumors spread that the foundering of the *Sindia* was caused by negligence. Both captain and crew were accused of intoxica-

*Sindia* wreckage became impromptu beach attractions for many years afer the wreck.

tion, celebrating the coming Christmas holiday while on duty.

On February 7, 1902, the captain and first mate faced a British Admiralty Court of Inquiry in Philadelphia. Although they denied all charges, the first mate, George Stewart, was found to have been negligent and drunk, and McKenzie was ruled to have "failed to exercise proper and seamanlike care and precaution."

Stewart's sailing papers were suspended for three months, McKenzie's for six. Reportedly broken in spirit, the captain returned to his native Scotland, where he died before his suspen-

sion time had elapsed.

Although all of the men aboard the vessel were saved, the ship was fated to retire from duty on the Ocean City surf. However, even before an attempt to return the ship to free waters was made, the removal of cargo was begun.

New York underwriters took charge of the stranded vessel and a wrecking company was employed to unload the cargo. Insurance covered about half of the million-dollar loss, and some of the water-soaked matting was taken to New York where it sold at a fraction of its value.

An enterprise calling itself the Sindia Co. bought the ship and remaining cargo for $5,500, then resold it to the Eavenson Naphtha Borax Soap Co. of Camden for $10,000.

Legal ownership of the *Sindia* had little to do with the final disposition of a large amount of its salvageable cargo, though. Almost immediately following abandonment of the ship, the pilferage began.

Matting, bamboo, curios, vases, even camphor oil became saleable commodities in Ocean City. A "Sindia Shop" was opened on the boardwalk to merchandise remnants of the ship's cargo. Counterfeit *Sindia* relics also were sold as souvenirs.

Many of the more interesting and valuable curios, along with the ship's figurehead, are housed in the Ocean City Historical Museum's Sindia Room, where they and pictures of the ship may be viewed by the public.

Several enterprising persons have tried in vain to gain access to the rest of the cargo. Each time a passage to a cargo hold has been created, sand has quickly filled the void.

Former Ocean City lifeguard Jim Macallister's memories of the devastating 1944 hurricane include a personal encounter with the legendary ship.

"By about 9:00 that night, the storm had abated and it was a gorgeous, crystal-clear night," Macallister recalled. "And I was always in awe of the mast of the *Sindia*, which had been standing up on 18th Street beach. Up on top of that big mast, there were three boards that formed a crow's nest, and they were beautiful, old wood, but nobody could ever get up to them to steal them.

"I just wondered if that hurricane had knocked that big mast down, so I took a walk down the beach that night and, sure enough, the hurricane had knocked the big mast down and the crow's nest was lying right there at my feet," he said. "There were still some old bolts holding it together, but I pulled them off.

"I put the boards under the front steps of the building in which I was living, and left them there for the rest of the season," he said. "I only took one board home with me at the end of the season, and I kept it in my basement for quite a few years. When they formed the Historical Society at Fourth and Wesley, I brought this board down and told them it was from the *Sindia,* and it's hanging right over the door in the museum today."

With the passage of time and the processes of nature, the impressive vessel eventually sank beneath the sands of the beach between 16th and 17th streets. As of the 1960s, the tops of the rudder post and tiller were visible at low tide, and a marker on the boardwalk indicates the great ship's location. The spot has been declared an historic site by the state of New Jersey.

## CHAPTER SEVENTEEN

# *Too Close for Comfort*

Not all of the shipwrecks occurring in the waters off Peck's Beach were the consequence of faulty navigation or storms. Many vessels fell victim to the weaponry of enemies with which the United States found itself at war, particularly in this century. New Jerseyans who look back on the two world wars as military struggles "over there" would be surprised to discover the action which took place just off the state's beaches.

The first days of June, 1918, introduced the ships sailing along the Jersey coast to a new maritime danger: the Unterseeboots of the Kaiser. At that time, according to David Seibold and Charles

*During World War II, a tower was constructed on the Music Pier for spotting submarines and aircraft.*

Adams in *Shipwrecks Off Ocean City,* a group of four German U-boats took up residence in area waters, launching a barrage of sneak attacks on American ships.

The *Edna, Hattie Dunn, Wappaug, Winneconne, Samuel W. Hathaway, Jacob* H. *Haskell, City of Columbus, Herbert L. Pratt —*

all were among the steamers and schooners downed by German submarines during that first week in June. On the *Edward H. Cole,* sailing along the New Jersey shoreline on June 2, someone saw the conning tower of a submarine in the waters ahead. Thinking it was an American vessel, the captain shouted, "We are

Americans." The reply was: "We are Germans."

The German captain then explained that the ship was to be blown up and that the passengers had ten minutes to debark. After the *Cole's* crew had rowed a safe distance away, the ship was sunk.

The pattern was often repeated. The *Texel* was a 5,000-ton freighter which the United States had transformed into a wartime supply transport. On a trip from Puerto Rico to New York City, it was greeted with two warning shots across its bow as a U-boat surfaced beside it.

The commander of the sub boarded the ship with some of his men. He was described by eyewitnesses as being quite courteous, extending his hand to the *Texel's* captain. He then explained, "Captain, I'm sorry to do this, but it must be. You will please clear your vessel as soon as possible, for we are going to blow her up." All hands abandoned ship, and the *Texel* was destroyed. There was no loss of life, for all thirty-five crew members, after thirty-six hours in the lifeboats, landed safely in Atlantic City.

Victims of German sneak attacks were not always allowed to depart in lifeboats. In the case of the *Isabel B. Wiley*, a 779-ton wooden schooner, the captain and his small crew were held as prisoners on a German submarine. After the Germans boarded the craft and gave notice that the *Wiley* would be sunk after the crew had left, the Americans were ushered down inside the U-boat, where they met forty one other prisoners from three other American ships.

After a week had passed, the sub came within sight of oncoming ships and released the prisoners so they could be rescued. Captain H. Thomassen of the *Wiley* recalled that the Germans had spent the time trying to convince the prisoners of the strength and prowess of the German Navy and the futility of resistance. By the end of the week, however, attitudes had mellowed, and almost every prisoner was given a souvenir from the sub upon leaving.

In addition to the direct threat of the German U-boats, their very presence intensified the danger of another already formidable enemy of the sailor: fog. In May, 1918, wartime regulations along the East Coast required ships to travel with lights dimmed. The report filed by company officials of the Savannah Lines' *City of Athens* indicates that the liner was complying with those regulations as it passed through the fog along the Ocean City shoreline on its way to Savannah, Ga., with 135 people on board.

Visibility was next to zero, so with no warning at all, the port bow of the *Athens* was ripped apart when the ship collided with

---

*The commander of the sub boarded the ship with some of his men. He was described by eyewitnesses as being quite courteous, extending his hand to the Texel's captain. He then explained, "Captain, I'm sorry to do this, but it must be. You will please clear your vessel as soon as possible, for we are going to blow her up."*

---

the French warship *La Glorie*. Within seven minutes the injured *Athens* had sunk, taking with it sixty seven lives. Passengers, most already asleep in their staterooms, were taken unawares, and most of the lifeboats had been overturned by the initial ramming.

The dilemma which World War I captains faced in trying to defend their ships against both the Unterseeboots and the fog was again a problem during World War II. In 1942, the Nazi U-boats were already in coastal waters and had torpedoed a number of ships not far from the shore.

As in World War I, the Navy ordered all ships to dim their lights. The *Santa Elisa* and the *San Jose* were among the ships which complied. Consequently, in January, 1942, they did not see each other until it was too late. The *San Jose* sunk before help arrived. The larger *Santa Elisa,* though still afloat, caught fire with its cargo of oil fueling the flames.

The Coast Guard from Ocean City aided in the rescue, and all crewmen were saved. Many needed medical treatment for exposure to the cold.

Sailing vessels had reason to be on guard. The authors of *Shipwrecks Off Ocean City* note an estimated 400 ships sank at the hands of Nazi U-boats. One of the earliest casualties was the *Varanger.*

A tanker headed for New York City with a cargo of oil in January 1942, the *Varanger* was about 28 miles off Ocean City when it was torpedoed. The *modus operandi* of the Nazi U-boat captains was not the same as their World War I counterparts. The first torpedo hit the *Varanger* at 3:00 a.m. — no warning shots, no offer of time to allow passengers and crew to abandon ship.

In spite of this, all forty one crew members reached their lifeboats. From that position, they watched two submarines surface and survey the wreckage. They kept silent, lest the Nazis open fire on the lifeboats. After four hours at sea, they drifted to the Sea Isle City shore, where they were aided by city residents.

The *Burrows* was a 7,600-ton freighter carrying a cargo of coal to New York City. As it passed only eight miles from Ocean City's beaches, it was struck by a torpedo from the *U-404*. After two more torpedoes, the *Burrows* was lost, as were twenty of its crew.

Fourteen men survived. The *U-404* met its own end about one year later, in North Atlantic waters. There were no survivors.

Stories still circulate of undiscovered German U-boats sunk offshore during the second world war. There are at least two of

---

*Captain H. Thomassen of the Wiley recalled that the Germans had spent the time trying to convince the prisoners of the strength and prowess of the German Navy and the futility of resistance. By the end of the week, however, attitudes had mellowed, and almost every prisoner was given a souvenir from the sub upon leaving.*

---

these, one, it is said, off Atlantic City, and the other off Cape May. Some divers refer to them as the diver's Holy Grail.

The tales of sunken ships off Ocean City are varied. Some are historically reliable while others, local fishermen will tell you, are more legend than fact. Still, true or not, each enhances the romance which people associate with the sea which borders this island home.

# CHAPTER EIGHTEEN

# Simon Lake: Submarine Pioneer

Considering the number of American ships sunk by German submarines off Ocean City's shore, it is ironic that an inventor of the underwater vessel was a member of the family that founded the city. Simon Lake was a grandson of the man by the same name who mortgaged his farm to finance development of the island. Like his namesake, Simon was willing to invest his money and energies in a project in which he believed.

A dreamer who made his imagination serve the practical, Lake was an inventor who in the course of his life patented a prefabricated house, under-river tunnel systems and a successful submarine. The latter became his obsession and, though the U.S. government largely ignored him, Lake planned and built subs for several countries around the world.

As a young man, Simon was considered a bit of a laggard by his elders, who criticized his daydreaming on the job at his father John and uncle Ezra's factory in Ocean City. The shade-roller manufacturing company started in Philadelphia in 1874, then moved to Toms River where it opened a foundry to make roller fittings. In 1883, the company relocated the foundry at 10th Street and West Avenue in the growing town on Peck's Beach.

In Ocean City, the company employed between 25 and 50 men and manufactured stove-lid lifters, wagon jacks and other castings, including the shade-roller fittings. Simon learned much about iron working at the plant and commuted to and from Philadelphia to study mechanical drawing.

Lake's father shared with him a faith in innovation and, when Simon invented a single-screw steering gear, the two men moved to Baltimore and began its manufacture, establishing a company named the J.C. Lake and Son Co. Shortly thereafter they invented a winder for dredging ships and Simon created a machine for capping cans capable of servicing 50,000 cans a day.

In 1893, the U.S. Navy advertised for designs for a submarine torpedo boat. Simon, whose curiosity had been tantalized by Jules Verne's *Twenty Thousand Leagues Under the Sea,* submitted his plans for a vessel to be called the *Argonaut* on June 3, 1893. The sub design included wheels on the bottom to enable it to ride like an automobile along the ocean floor and a diving compartment allowing crew members to enter and leave the ship underwater without adversely affecting cabin pressure.

Aside from the fact that the Navy had doubts about the possibility of building such a vessel, another inventor, John Holland, presented not only a design but a promise to build the subs. Consequently, the Holland Torpedo Boat Co. of Patterson, N.J., was awarded the contract.

Holland himself was an interesting character. An Irish-American with strong ties to the Irish Republican movement, he

*American Marines search crewmen of the German submarine U-858, captured 50 miles offshore Cape May on May 10, 1945. Simon Lake never intended for his invention to be used for war; his earliest working submarine was built for exploration.*

first intended his underwater fighting vessel to be used by his radical friends on the Emerald Isle.

The American Fenian Society, of which Holland was a member, was a predecessor of American organizations that support the Irish Republican Army in its struggle to free Ireland from British domination. The word *fenian* comes from the same root as that of the name of the political arm of the IRA, *Sinn Fein* (pronounced shin fane), which means "ourselves alone" — that is, without the British.

After a series of political assassinations that weakened their support at home and in America, the Fenians disbanded after a few short years, although the Irish Republican Brotherhood continued to prepare for revolution. But because of the dissolution of the American wing, Holland's dream of sinking British ships with submarine torpedo boats was finished, and he successfully sold the U.S. government on the idea of including his invention in its arsenal.

Unfortunately, because of time constraints written into the contract, Holland failed to complete his end of the bargain and he abandoned the project in 1900. This did not clear the way for Simon Lake, however, for despite Holland's failure, congressional

---

*As a young man, Simon was considered a bit of a laggard by his elders, who criticized his daydreaming on the job at his father John and uncle Ezra's factory in Ocean City.*

---

appropriations for submarines carried the language "Holland boats exclusively," and even after Lake was able to secure an agreement of sale from the Navy should he build the subs himself, the Senate endorsed it but the House killed the plan.

The irony of these events lies in the fact that Lake was able to interest several other governments in his submarine and finally sold it to the Russians, then under the czar. When war broke out between Russia and Japan just before World War I, the Lake submarine became the first effective fighting submarine to be used in battle.

When other governments including Italy and Germany tried to employ Lake, the Russians offered him 5 million rubles to stay in St. Petersburg, where he lived and worked under the alias E. Simons. Nevertheless, Lake returned to the United States and built his own shipyard at Bridgeport, Conn., eventually realizing his vision of building submarines for his own country.

Although clearly a success in accomplishing his goals, Lake earned and lost several fortunes, always willing to reinvest his capital gains in new schemes of innovation. When he died in 1945, he was not a rich man; foreign governments had acquired many of the secrets of his designs by espionage, and international patent rights were not adequately protected.

In any case, Lake never really intended his invention to be used for war. His earliest working submarine, the *Argonaut Jr.*, was built for exploration of the seas, and the greatest reward to the inventor was the commendation of his inspiration, Jules Verne, who telegraphed him, saying of the ship, "Her conspicuous success [will] push on underwater navigation all over the world." Verne, however, also carried the foreboding opinion that "the next great war may be largely a contest between submarine boats."

# CHAPTER NINETEEN

# *Religion and Real Estate*

*At the dawn of the 1900s, the island of Peck's Beach was still largly a sandy woodland.*

From the earliest days of the island's appearance on European maps, its destiny has been influenced by two primal impulses: to worship and to lay claim to land. Several Old World nations asserted rights over South Jersey, but English might won out and, through her grants, possession of the island eventually came into the hands of the West Jersey Society and was deeded to John Somers.

The first records show Richard Townsend of Cape May County bought 663 acres from the Society in 1726 for 46 pounds, 8 shillings, and 2 farthings. Land included in the deal was at the southwest end of the island.

Townsend, the first white child born in the county, was a cattle raiser on the mainland about ten miles south of the island. When he died, he left the property to his two sons, who sold it in 1755 for 180 pounds, a 400 percent profit in only twenty nine years. The first real estate killing had been made, a tradition as intrinsic to the history of the island as the foundation of the Tabernacle.

Beach property had risen in value when the Townsend boys sold their holdings because cattle no longer were allowed to graze freely on the mainland where settlements were being established, and the islands were a natural pen, uninhabited and surrounded by water.

*An Ocean City real estate auction is held in a large tent, as were the first religious services on the island.*

Even the choice of Peck's Beach for the Lake brothers' Christian retreat was determined by real estate considerations. They first selected the section of Absecon Island later to become Margate, but were unable to take full possession of the property because some of it was legally owned by minors unable to sign a contract of sale. So they focused across the inlet on Peck's Beach. From that point on, the original religious purpose of founding a Christian seaside resort became inextricable from dealings in real estate.

By mortgaging his Pleasantville farm in 1879, Simon Lake came up with the $10,000 needed to buy the entire island in order to write into each deed restrictions prohibiting alcohol sales and Sunday commerce. The February 27 minutes of the Ocean City

Association, formed by the Lakes and their colleagues, explain that the organization at first considered leasing its property (as was done in Ocean Grove to ensure adherence to its religious laws), but finally settled upon the deed restrictions.

What had begun as a "holy experiment" in 1879, with the founding of the Ocean City Association, quickly became a real

*Three beachfront houses stand in otherwise undeveloped land at 30th and West Streets in 1907. Workers constructing the water tower, facing page, paused for the camera but the development of the island never broke pace once it had begun.*

estate venture. The association's board of managers was formed on November 19 of that year to handle its affairs. It was determined that the nine board members would include three Methodist ministers, three Methodist ministers or laymen, and three "members or nonmembers of the Methodist Episcopal Church." The group's first move was to announce the sale of $10 shares of association stock. One hundred thousand dollars of capital stock was issued.

Five hundred shares were sold in January of 1880. Isaac Smith, who bought 50 shares at that time, soon moved to the island and constructed the Ocean House Hotel, Ocean City's first, later renamed the Hotel Brighton.

That first hotel was built on what was then beachfront property costing $125 for each of four lots, a tidy investment, considering the value of similar property on the island today.

At that time, lots on West Avenue corners were priced at $50, inside lots at $25; Asbury Avenue corner lots cost $75, inside lots $50; Central Avenue corners cost $125, while inside ones went for $100; Wesley Avenue corner lots were $150, inside properties $125; Ocean Avenue corners were $200, inside lots $150; and Atlantic Avenue corner lots brought $200, inside ones $150.

In order to further the development of the new colony, the

association needed to take legal possession of the entire island and attract like-minded individuals to the project. The former problem proved more difficult than the founders expected.

Because titles to some portions of the island were vague concerning amounts of acreage, the transfer of a particular deed did not insure against legal challenge by owners of bordering property. This was especially true of those who held "grazing rights" to pasture land, passed from generation to generation without adequate documentation.

The Rev. Ezra Lake soon found himself devoting much of his time and energy to the task of untangling the webs of competing claims to what was then nearly worthless land. The process was successfully completed after four arduous years.

Nevertheless, by 1880, details had been worked out sufficiently for the association to sell 508 lots for a total of $85,000. They also set aside lots for what are now the Tabernacle grounds, between Fifth and Sixth streets and Asbury and Wesley avenues, and for religious and public facilities, including a summer home for orphans, a church and a school. Regulations concerning sales of building lots rested with the association, and as early as 1881 the association was buying advertising in the fledgling *Ocean City Sentinel* to announce their availability.

It is astonishing to consider the number of buildings constructed by the fourth year of the community's existence: 112 houses, twenty six barns and stables, four hotels, three general stores, three restaurants, three public bathhouses, three lifesaving stations, four comfort stations, two real estate offices, two meat markets, two public halls, two photograph galleries, an auditorium (Tabernacle), a bakery, public school, drug store, barber shop, post office, paint shop, wheelwright shop, blacksmith shop, printing office, coal yard, lumberyard and lime, brick and mortar firm.

One of the first advertising vehicles for the resort real estate was not in the least shy of marketing religion and land in the same breath. *The Ocean City Guide Book and Directory* printed an ad signed by the Rev. Ezra Lake in 1893 that called Ocean City a "moral seaside resort, not excelled as a health restorer" and stated that lovers of temperance and morals should join in its vision. Further down the column, it made its pitch: "Thousands of lots for sale at various prices, located in all parts of the city."

*This view of the beach is dominated by the Brighton Hotel, which opened in 1881, at 7th Street.*

*In its earliest days, Ocean City's charm was on display in everyday activities.*

The same edition of *The Guide Book* listed early residents Robert Fisher and William Lake as selling, of course, lots, cottages and oceanfront sites for building. Although what was oceanfront then is midtown now, the pattern was set for environmental crises still facing Ocean City today.

In June of 1880, the association appointed a committee to find out if the state was willing to sell riparian (beach access) rights around the island and at what price. On December 28, it announced it had received an answer: "The state Riparian Commission [has] granted the Association permission to purchase riparian rights at the rate of twenty five cents per foot for the oceanfront, which would include the right to the bayfront."

In February of 1881, the association resolved to rent the ocean-front on a per-foot basis for beach privileges. Looking back at that resolution, beach tags seem pretty mild stuff.

Florence Leeds Block of the Cape May County Historical and Genealogical Society points out that at that time many people bought oceanfront lots from the association only to have the ocean add substantial amounts of new beach to the seaward side of the island. Visitors to the Brighton Hotel, originally at Seventh Street and the beach, once had been able to fish from its porch — by 1940, when the edifice was razed, it was a full three blocks from the beach.

Real estate sales boomed those first few years, and a comparison of prices of lots in 1880 with those in 1881 demonstrates just how much land appreciation took place. A corner lot on Wesley Avenue in 1880, for instance, sold for $150; by the following year that price had leaped to $1,000. Central Avenue corner lots that went for $125 in the former year appreciated to $700 in the latter. Properties on the other streets rose in value at the same rate. Prices were contingent on the buyer's fulfillment of a promise to build a cottage worth double the price of the land.

One problem the association encountered in its accelerated real estate business was its inability to keep track of everything that changed hands. It had spent a good deal of money just buying up all of the property on the island, and a number of people, it was found, had stopped their payments after handing over the ten-percent down payment. The association's cash flow was also hurt by its practice of exchanging land for goods, services and interest on stockholders' shares in the association in lieu of cash. The association's board of managers found that by September, 1881, they not only had nothing in store, they actually were overdrawn at the bank by $23.97, due in part to uncollected balances from real estate sales.

Besides crippling normal debit-credit recording, the use of land in lieu of cash made it nearly impossible to keep tabs on property

buyers. The bewildered book-keeper, Charles Mathews Jr., a real estate broker himself, resigned his position and sold his shares of stock in the association in April of 1883. Apparently, Mathews simply was unable to translate the eccentric financial records of the early years into a workable accounting system.

However, the religious motivations which began this venture did show through the dust of the maddening rush to sell land and recoup losses. Ministers of Protestant denominations initially received a fifty-percent discount on the price of one lot, providing they were active in the ministry.

That favored status, created in March, 1880, was amended in August of the same year to restrict sale of the lots by those ministers to those upon which buildings had been erected. All others were required to pay the association the cash difference between what they paid and the regular price.

Finally, by October, 1881, the association retracted its offer of bargain prices to clergy, although it did provide for a fifty-percent mortgage at six percent interest, the mortgage to be considered discharged after a house was erected on the lot.

Real estate always has been the most vigorous industry in Ocean City, beginning with the founders' decision to sell rather than lease lots as had been done in Ocean Grove.

The curious mixture of real estate development and religion is as old as the town itself. The Puritan principles of good business sense combined with pietism were fundamental to the founders' thinking and activity. An old map of the island hanging in the Ocean City Historical Museum today is bordered by advertise-ments for real estate sales and related services with names as familiar as Lake and Fisher.

Land investments really began to boom in the 1920s, though, a time when many kinds of speculation thrived. A number of hotels and even vacant lots greatly appreciated in value.

There are countless examples of skyrocketing land prices. A

property between First Street and St. Charles Place was sold for $88,000 in 1925 and resold three days later for $120,000. An adjoining property was sold separately for $79,000, resold for $88,500 and sold six hours later for $97,000. Although the first sale took place earlier that summer, by August 7 of the same year, it was advertised for $135,000.

A lot at North Street and Stenton Place was sold three times in one day. A realtor sold it for $68,000, bought it back for $78,500 and sold it again for $110,000.

Nevertheless, in the midst of such gross inflation, at least one man resisted, foreshadowing the gutsy inflexibility of Atlantic City residents who refused to sell their often ramshackle homes to the casino industry at astronomical prices.

Captain James Lee, an early resident, bought an Asbury Avenue lot and built a home and store on it around 1880 at a time when shorefront lots sold for an estimated $125. In 1925 he was first offered $50,000 and then told to name his price by a land speculator. He refused the offer, saying he didn't want to cheat the man.

In 1929, the stock market crash burst the bubbles of investors and speculators in all areas of the economy, including land sales, and an animated real estate market was devastated in Ocean City as elsewhere.

A town which appeared in the early 1920s to be on its way to enormous economic health and development became so depressed by the end of the decade that many people had to move away to find jobs. Not until the post-war era would this trend be fully reversed.

After World War II, Ocean City and its real estate market experienced a boom which has had only minor setbacks since. The popularity of seaside resort homes and the ability to purchase property on which to build them have continued to grow during the past 40 years.

Only in the mid-'70s, when inflated interest rates and tight financing limited the numbers of people able to buy vacation properties, did the local real estate business feel the pinch of bad economic times. Since that time, however, the market has continued on a positive track.

New zoning laws surely will affect not only the types of buildings that will be erected on the island but the number of dwelling units — that is, density. Still, the laws of supply and demand will win out. For better or worse, Ocean City is limited in size and natural resources. And the demand to live on the island seems to grow each year. The city's proximity to the booming Atlantic City casino industry certainly hasn't hurt.

Whatever the specific character of land development that takes place over the next generation, it's probably safe to say that investment in Ocean City will continue to be rewarding.

*The Burleigh Cottages, built in 1894, on Central Avenue.*

# CHAPTER TWENTY

# *Shuttling to the Shore*

*The Beesley's Point bridge, built for automobiles, opened in 1928 with a grand procession.*

Living on an island makes transportation a serious concern, and so it has been since the founding of Ocean City. Even before the town was developed, farmers who used the meadows as grazing land needed to drive their cattle across Great Egg Harbor Bay either at the south end where the channel was narrow or from the Somers Point area where Cowpens Island served as a resting point for the alternately swimming and wading stock.

Parker Miller, the only permanent resident of Peck's Beach at the time the Ocean City Association was formed, had "made a sort of mudbank walk from the Bay shore to his house," according to survey team member Robert Fisher. This was the first manmade approach to the island proper. The mudbank, which was built near present-day Seventh Street, was not considered a desirable landing point, however, so a wharf was built around Fourth Street.

In the *First Annual Report of the President of the Ocean City Association,* the Rev. William Wood described the work that had been accomplished in installing the wharf.

*Somers Point was connected to Philadelphia by rail, via Pleasantville, in 1880, but to get to the island from Somers Point passengers needed to take the ferry boats.*

and setting them down on dry land. Fisher's journal testifies to the comedy sometimes surrounding this unusual form of travel.

"Captain Amos Lewis took off his boots, rolled up his pants and got overboard to back his passengers ashore; one by one he toted them slipping and sliding over the mud — those in the back like to split at those being carried, and those that had gotten ashore laughing at those whose turn came next," Fisher explained.

"When all but one was landed he also prepared for the trip but was so full of laughter at the comical situation that he could scarcely control himself or keep his seat on the back of his carrier; still he would utter words of caution and tell how little he desired mud baptism.

"We have built a wharf 125 feet long by 72 feet wide, on our Bay front, high enough to be above the storm tides," he wrote. "We have constructed a good road over the meadow, about 1,000 feet, from the wharf to the streets of the City."

At high tide, travelers to the island could land easily at the site of the wharf, but when the waters lowered, it was necessary to wade from the boats to the bay shore. Some boat captains obliged the landing parties by carrying them on their backs from the boat

"When they got pretty well toward shore, the captain's foot slipped and the dominie was dumped heels over head in the mud," he continued. "The tall hat flew several yards ahead of him while the safe ones on the shore laughed uproariously at the plight of their friend."

Even walking on the island could be fraught with difficulties at the turn of the century. Journalist Ginna Block remembers an uncle's tales of the days when walking from the downtown district to the south end could be a serious proposition.

"My uncle told me that back in the early 1900s, down around 50th street, there was a stream," she said, "and he used to reminisce about having to wait several times for low tide to complete his walk back to the south end. There were quite a few streams cutting across the island, but the one in the south end you couldn't get through at high tide, so if you wanted to go downtown, you had to watch the tides."

Street development began on the island almost immediately after the city's founding.

"The fact that Mr. (Parker) Miller's House was the only place where any entertainment could be had, made it necessary to have some means of reaching it," Fisher wrote in 1880, and so "Asbury Avenue was the first to be opened." Numbered streets were cleared down to Eighth Street, and West, Asbury, Central and Wesley all had been laid by year's end. Also during that first year, arrangements were made for the graveling of sidewalks and streets.

The first highway to the island, called "the turnpike," was opened in 1883 and connected the south end to Beesley's Point. The project cost about $6,000. Ocean City Association President W. B. Wood described the two-mile road, saying that the bay "is spanned by a good bridge, containing a draw, at which is erected a suitable house for the accommodation of the toll keeper."

Although built for horse and buggies, the turnpike was accommodating automobiles by 1906, when only 20 cars and one motorcycle were registered by city motorists. Even then, the chief of police, Samuel B. Scull, found it necessary to issue a warning to young drivers that strict adherence to speed limits would be enforced.

*The first Pennsylvania Railroad train to arrive in Ocean City, at 17th Street, 1897.*

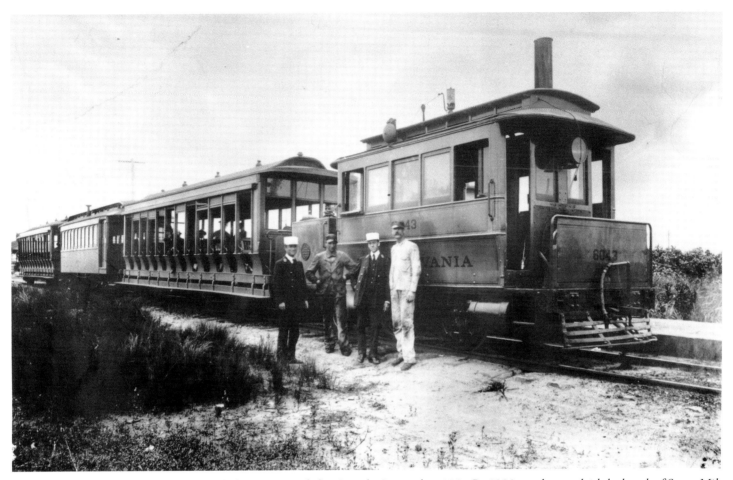

*Rail service between Ocean City and Tuckahoe was extended to Sea Isle City in the 1880s. By 1889, tracks were laid the length of Seven Mile Beach (Avalon and Stone Harbor) and commuter service began on a line the became known as the Yellow Kid, above.*

Even without the traffic jams between Philadelphia and the shore resorts motorists now face, a drive to the Ocean City area in the early part of the century could be hazardous. Not everyone was infatuated with the new-fangled automobile, and the contraptions were so notorious for disturbing the peace that one Philadelphia newspaper in 1904 suggested that police in the towns between Philadelphia and the shore shoot the tires out from under the noisier autos if they became too bothersome.

The bridges and highway linking Ocean City to Somers Point, built in 1913-14, were rebuilt in 1932-33 and named a memorial to Ocean City's World War I veterans, Souvenir coins of the dedication, on August 19, 1933, feature the drawbridge on one side

*Electric trolley cars transported people from the garden section in the north to 59th Street at the south end between 1895 and 1929. Facing page: A postcard image from the 1920s showed Ocean City's automobile and trolley bridges, along with a sailing option.*

and the *Sindia* on the other.

While access to the bayfront and interior of the island was in place early in the town's history, from the beginning, the city's founders sought to provide convenient transportation for Philadelphia-area pilgrims from the railroad station in Pleasantville, and this, too, was achieved by the time the first annual report was issued early in 1881.

"Through our active efforts, a Rail Road Company has been organized, known as the Pleasantville and Ocean City R.R. Co., and a first-class rail road built for a distance of between seven and eight miles, from Pleasantville to Somers Point, and is now in complete

running order, making regular trips daily," Wood reported.

The intention of facilitating visits from Philadelphia to Ocean City is clear in the report's subsection, "How to Reach it."

"Take 'Philadelphia and Atlantic City Railroad' at Pier No.8, South Delaware Avenue or 'West Jersey Railroad' at Market Street wharf," the report directs the potential visitor. "Both connect at Pleasantville with the 'Pleasantville and Ocean City Railroad.' The fare is low, and several trains a day are run. You can go down in the morning, have several hours at the seaside, and return same day. Round trip tickets are sold, good cars furnished, and good time made."

The newly established Pleasantville and Ocean City Railroad Co. did not bring travellers across the bay to the island. For that, a steamboat was provided. In 1880, the vessel brought passengers across the bay from Somers Point five times daily.

Nevertheless, from the earliest days, the Ocean City Association intended to secure direct and complete rail service to its Christian resort. By 1885, when the association president's *Fourth Annual Report* was published, the group's frustration in realizing this goal was evident.

"Notwithstanding all our efforts and expectations we were doomed to disappointment," the report states. "The railroad officials were satisfied with our propositions and offers of cooperation, but there was a hitch somewhere. We must wait a little longer. Our only consolation is it cannot be much longer. Our increasing travel and population demand the railroad, though the natural obstacles and cost of its construction may defer it for a time."

An agreement between the town and one of several competing railroad companies was struck in early 1884, but full rail service was not in operation until November of that year. The city paid for grading, building a depot and a railroad bridge across the meadows from Tuckahoe to hasten completion of the project.

*A steamboat docks at the Second Street wharf with passengers from Longport in 1911. Facing page: The Pennsylvania Railroad station at Eighth Street and West Avenue in 1930.*

By the end of the century, the line between Tuckahoe and Ocean City had been extended to Sea Isle City. Railroad tracks for the Sea Isle-Ocean City route were laid along West Avenue, because the West Jersey Railroad Co. turned down the association's offer of Simpson Avenue for the line. Finally, in 1889, tracks were laid the length of Seven Mile Beach, including Stone Harbor and Avalon, and the connection was completed between this line and Sea Isle City. The commuter train that made the run between Stone Harbor and Ocean City became affectionately known as "the Yellow Kid."

The board of managers financed the Ocean City part of the project, forming what was known as the Ocean City Railroad Co. by selling 10 blocks of undeveloped land between 23rd and 33rd streets. The sale raised $40,000 to contribute toward the

$70,000 cost of constructing the line. Ocean City's assumption of construction costs was part of the agreement between the board and West Jersey Railroad.

Access to the island from the north in the early days was facilitated by steamboat service from Longport. From 1894 to 1918, the Camden and Atlantic Railroad's steamboats carried commuters from the 16th Street wharf in Longport to Second Street in Ocean City, where a wharf had beep built by the West Jersey Railroad. Regular steamboat service was provided only during the summer season, from about June 15 to September 15.

A trolley system running from the steamboat wharf at Second Street and the bay began running in 1893, first as far south as 16th Street, but later to 59th. Although it initially provided only summer service, by 1915 it was running all year. During the

tourist season, a traveler could catch a trolley every 15 minutes, but in the colder months only one round trip a day was made to take workers and school children back and forth.

Robert B. Chew of Haddonfield, N.J., became general manager of the trolley line in 1913, and there was never such a crafty overseer. Ever wary of those potentially dishonest employees who might pocket some of the five-cent fares, Chew favored young applicants who still lived with their parents and didn't need the money. He eyed suspiciously those who wanted to be money-collecting conductors. Applicants with the best chances of getting the job were those who neither needed nor wanted it — a curious employment practice, but obviously an effective one, for Chew remained in his job until the trolley line closed down in 1929.

In 1934, the rail line from the mainland to Sea Isle, Avalon, Stone Harbor, Strathmere and Ocean City was eliminated, although service from Tuckahoe to Ocean City was continued. Buses transported patrons from the southerly towns to Cape May Court House or Ocean City train stations.

*Two Pennsylvania Railroad locomotives idle at the Ocean City station.*

In 1960, the Pennsylvania-Reading Seashore Lines, now handling all rail service in the area, asked the Public Utility Commission for permission to end its runs from Camden and Philadelphia to Ocean City, Atlantic City, Wildwood, Cape May, Hammonton and Millville. The following year, they were permitted to eliminate 15 weekly trains, 17 Saturday trains and 11 Sunday trains, seriously limiting access by rail to the southern shore communities.

Increases both in the use of cars and buses and in the price of railroad tickets contributed to the end of rail service to Ocean City in 1981. The only remaining train service to the southern New Jersey shore is to Atlantic City from Philadelphia.

# CHAPTER TWENTY-ONE

# *In and Out of the National Spotlight*

Interwoven into the fabric of Ocean City history are many minor stories that are removed from its major themes but nevertheless add to its texture. Some are human interest, some eccentricities of the town, while others are of little-known individuals, but all brought the resort flashes of public notice.

Among these is the story of a stray dog named Hobo. First found in a snowdrift in 1920, the little canine was rescued by a humane couple and later adopted by the entire town.

Until his death in 1936, the furry vagabond strolled the boardwalk as if it were his territory, and the fuss made over him by townspeople, summer residents and visitors soon showed in his metamorphosis from a straggly stray into a roly-poly butterball. Even in the wintertime, he maintained his portly carriage, fed by shop owners and restaurateurs among whom he made daily rounds.

When Hobo died of old age, a newspaper reporter began a fund-raising campaign to finance a doggy drinking fountain memorializing the community pet. First erected on the high school lawn, the fountain eventually was moved to the grounds of the Ocean City Historical Museum at 409 Wesley Ave. where it now stands.

*During the Depression, Ocean City issued its own scrip to pay city employees.*

*Marshall Earl Reid was sworn in as a deputy mail carrier to make one of the 31 experimental airmail flights in 1912. He flew from Stone Harbor to Ocean City in 29 minutes.*

interesting copy for columnists around the nation.

Even the 1986 political battle to abolish the blue law made its way into headlines and onto network news programs. Among the numerous stories sure to become local legends are those of customers and merchants being fined for buying and selling apparently innocent merchandise.

Among them was boardwalk merchant Edward Devlin, fined for buying uncut cantaloupes: cut ones were perfectly legal, and Devlin wanted to dramatize the absurdity of the contradictions under the law. A local delicatessen owner was arrested when her employee sold a plainclothes policeman a package of frozen steaks.

Campaign signs for and against the blue law: sprouted up on lawns all over town.

The story of Hobo hit the Philadelphia press and was immediately picked up by the wire services, which sent it to papers throughout the country.

Less attractive characterizations of Ocean City sprang from the town's dedication to traditions which many Americans found curiously outdated. Sunday-closing laws and prohibitions against alcohol sales — both passed down by the city's founders — made

After dark, though, pro-blue law night riders in a mysterious red pickup truck were seen snitching anti-blue-law signs from people's yards. The now-comic tales are endless and are sure to become material for yarns people will tell their grandchildren about Ocean City in the good old days.

In the November referendum that followed, the Sunday-closing ordinance was put aside, but the traditional values it represented to many citizens continue to be expressed in the family-oriented lifestyle of the town.

Ocean City folks are more comfortable with quiet Sundays, even with the legal restrictions gone, and prohibition against alcohol sales on the island remains intact. Both supporters and opponents of the abolished blue laws agree that the city's being a dry town is essential to its uniqueness as a family resort.

Ocean City's history not only is filled with a variety of interesting tidbits that at various times pushed the town into the national limelight, but it also contains a number of "firsts" for which it has received little notice.

On land, on sea, and in the air, as the saying goes, the island was the site of pioneering experimentation. Unlike some other small towns, like Kitty Hawk, N.C., Ocean City never gained a reputation as a historical site; nevertheless, it hosted events and produced men and women whose creativity helped further progress in a variety of fields.

For instance, few people know that one of the early submarines was invented by Simon Lake, a nephew of the Reverends Lake who founded the Christian resort on the island.

Fittingly, Ocean City also pioneered transport by air, in that it was the site of one of 31 experimental airmail flights commissioned by the U.S. Postal Service. In 1912, these flights were given the go-ahead, despite Congress's refusal to pay for them.

Marshall Earl Reid, sworn in as a deputy mail carrier, made the flight from Stone Harbor to Ocean City between August 3 and August 10, 1912. His hydroplane carried more than 500 pieces of mail in its 29-minute journey. During most of the flight, Reid's mechanic, Orton Hoover, piloted the plane.

Ocean City's reputed conservatism never stopped it from experimenting with what it considered to be good ideas. For example, on September 10, 1911, the municipality became the first New Jersey seashore resort to change from a City Council to

*Hobo, at age 18 in 1936, was the well-loved, overfed mascot of Ocean City. He gained national fame when the city memorialized him with a drinking fountain for pets following his demise.*

a City Commission form of government.

The move may have been prompted by the uncovering of corruption in the city government when it was learned that City Treasurer Ira S. Champion had forged financial documents, costing Ocean City about $10,000. In the wake of that disclosure, several former city officials admitted to having accepted commissions from companies doing business with the city.

The new form of government, introduced to respond to the apparent inadequacies in the council system, continued for 67 years after its inception. In 1978, the mayor-council form became the governmental method of Ocean City, and it has remained in

*A procession of automobiles crosses the new Beesley's Point Bridge, bannered with Old Glory, in June 1928. The line of traffic previewed things to come in later decades.*

effect ever since.

During the Great Depression, the town initiated another bold experiment. Money was so short in Ocean City that the municipality printed its own scrip, totaling $150,000, to pay its employees. The $1, $5 and $10 phony money was legal tender only for paying taxes to the city. Private businessmen were on their own in determining its redemptive value.

On March 17, 1933, city commissioners passed the resolution authorizing the issuance of the scrip by the city. The municipal money was actually promissory notes, accruing interest of four percent after June 1, 1933.

So successful was the experiment that within a few months, Cape May County itself issued scrip totaling $60,000, and several municipalities nearby Ocean City also followed its lead.

*The* Sindia *begins to disintegrate and sink deeper into the sand, several years after grounding — this photograph is circa 1903.*

# Epilogue

Perhaps never in its history has Ocean City stood at such a critical juncture concerning the direction its development will take. Initiatives to ensure that the ocean and bay waters will be cleaner and more healthful for ourselves and future generations have been prompted by warning signs nature has given us up and down the eastern seaboard. The tendency to build on every available bit of ground on the island is being reconsidered as a result of the problems that have accompanied growing density. Also, the erosion of the city's beaches through storms and other natural processes has presented a challenge to geologists and engineers.

However, the people who today make Ocean City their home have embarked on a new course to correct problems that exist. Living by and from the sea and bay, residents are directly and through their representatives searching for ways to clean up whatever polluting agents may lie offshore. They are working to solve the problems of waste disposal, limited drinking water reservoirs and crowded construction. Like our many visitors, we, too, love the invigorating smell of the salt air and the succulent taste of food drawn fresh from clear and pure salt water — and we want to keep them that way.

The erosion problem also is being addressed with modern technology and old-fashioned good sense. Efforts to protect the beaches date back to Ocean City's early days. The *First Annual Report of the Ocean City Association* in 1880 states that during the first year of the city's development "hundreds of loads of brushwood" were carted to the oceanfront near the inlet "for the purpose of gathering the moving sand in that locality, and thus extending our Ocean frontage."

Simon Lake, father of three of the city's founders, may have been the first casualty in the perpetual struggle to preserve the beaches from the destructive power of the sea. Three years after the city's founding, Simon was experimenting with ways to pile brush to seed dunes. When the axe he was using slipped, he cut off his foot, developed blood poisoning and died on November 28, 1881.

Although technology has developed a great deal since Lake's day, the principle upon which he based his efforts continues to be considered the most sound. Retrospective of that first effort to increase the size of the beach, resident conservationists still find natural methods of trapping and holding sand among the most effective means of preserving and enlarging the island's beaches. Now, as then, planting vegetation indigenous to the area has been preferred by the ecology-minded. Dune systems still are the best defense against beach erosion.

Part of the fascination people have with the sea is its ever-changing nature; it is always the same and always different. At the same time, this characteristic is the cause of enormous human frustration, as the ocean takes sand from one location and re-deposits it elsewhere. Dunes serve as a buffer, a last wall of resistance, preserving a measure of strand from natural erosion.

Lake knew that piling brush and then covering it with sand begins the process by which wind and water give back what they have taken from a beach. Whether he further observed the holding power of beach grass on dunes is unclear, but we may assume that, as astute an observer as he seemed to be, he probably would not have let that simple fact go unnoticed.

Aside from natural erosion, further submersion threatens our

*Ocean City's last railroad station at Tenth Street and Haven Avenue now is a bus terminal, but most visitors travel by automobile to "America's Greatest Family Resort."*

coast in this century. A warming trend in the earth's atmosphere, at least partly caused by excessive use of fossil fuels and fires in the equatorial forests, could, according to some scientists, result in the rise of the sea level by about a foot in the next forty years. Should this prediction be realized, about 125 feet of shoreline will end up under water.

Whatever happens, the people of Ocean City are not going to let go of their island easily. But instead of working against nature, as has been done in the past, we are learning that it is imperative to cooperate with her forces and rhythms.

Clearly, Ocean City no longer is the isolated New Eden the city's founders encountered when they landed on its shores. What it will become will be determined by its present caretakers, their vision of its future and reverence for its past.

*Tim Cain*
*Ocean City, NJ*
*1988*

# Acknowledgements

With special thanks to Mary Anne Haren, who was indispenable in the collection and sorting of research material and the organization and typing of the manuscript for this book. Also, with great appreciation to Harold Lee, dean of Ocean City historians, whose books must be a prime source for anyone writing about the island.

The following have provided encouragement and/or information, personally or through their writing, without which this effort would have been impossible:

William Ashmead
Atlantic County Historical Museum and Library
Gina Block
Joseph and Mary Cain
Elizabeth B. Carey
Margaret Kelly Conlan
Mary Cooper, Somers Mansion
Neely and Michael Crowley
Ed Davis
Edward Devlin III
Katherine Field
John Flood

Leslee Ganss
Katherine Schuff Hohman
Donald C. and Lizanne Kelly LeVine
Stanley Kops
James and Carol Macallister
Edna Streaker May
Ocean City Conservation Commission
Ocean City Historical Museum
Marth Parsons
Senior Studios
The Sentinel-Ledger
Gail Travers
Rick Travers

*Two scenes of Ocean City, near 8th Street and Asbury Avenue, when automobiles became commonplace.*

### Photographs and Illustrations

Atlantic City Free Public Library,
Heston Collection
Katherine Field
Marilyn Ganss

Katherine Schuff Hohman
Edna Streaker May
Ocean City Historical Museum
Senior Studios
Temple Universtiy Urban Archives/
Philadelphia Evening Bulletin

New Jersey State Police archives
New Jersey State Library
Library of Congress
US Army Corps of Engineers
National Archives

# *Bibliography*

Block, Florence Leeds. "Our Heritage" [as clipped and filed in the Cape May County Library, Cape May Court House, New Jersey].

Block, Ginna. "Recollections" series in *The Ocean City Record*. Ocean City, New Jersey, 1978-79.

Bruno, Karen. "Looking Backwards" series in *The SandPaper*. Ocean City, New Jersey, 1981-82.

Buchholz, Margaret Thomas, and Savadove, Larry. *Great Storms of the Jersey Shore*. West Creek, New Jersey: Down The Shore Publishing. 1993.

Buchholz, Margaret Thomas. *New Jersey Shipwrecks: 350 Years in the Graveyard of the Atlantic*. West Creek, New Jersey: Down The Shore Publishing. 2004.

_____. *Shore Chronicles: Diaries and Travelers' Tales from the Jersey Shore 1764-1955*. West Creek, New Jersey: Down The Shore Publishing. 1999.

Cape May County Chamber of Commerce. "History of Ocean City" [as clipped and filed in the Cape May County Library, Cape May Court House, New Jersey].

Casebeer, Janet. "Old Guards — Old Friends" in *The SandPaper*. Ocean City, New Jersey, August 20, 1987.

Cunningham, John T. *The New Jersey Shore*. New York: Rutgers University Press, 1958.

Darby, Bertram. "The Ocean City Story" in *The Cape May County Magazine* [as clipped and filed in the Cape May County Library, Cape May Court House, New Jersey].

Esposito, Frank J. *Travelling New Jersey*, 1978.

Farner, Thomas P. *New Jersey In History: Fighting to Be Heard*. Harvey Cedars, New Jersey: Down The Shore Publishing. 1996.

Gately, Bill. *Sentinels of the Shore: A Guide to the Lighthouses and Lightships of New Jersey*. West Creek, New Jersey: Down The Shore Publishing. 1998.

Handschuch, Dick, and Marino, Sal. *The Beach Bums Guide to the Boardwalks of New Jersey*. West Creek, New Jersey: Down The Shore Publishing. 2008.

Hathaway, Lucinda. *Takashi's Voyage: The Wreck of the Sindia*. West Creek, New Jersey: Down The Shore Publishing. 1995.

Heston, Alfred M. *Absegami: Annals of Eyren Haven and Atlantic City 1609-1904*. Published by the author, 1904.

Kirk, James B III. *Golden Light: The 1878 Diary of Captain Thomas Rose Lake*. West Creek, New Jersey: Down The Shore Publishing. 2003.?

League of Women Voters. *Know Your Town: Ocean City, New Jersey*. Ocean City, New Jersey, 1979.

Lee, Harold. "City of Ocean City" in *Tales of the Jersey Cape: Official Bicentennial Commemorative History of Cape May County*. Cape May Court House, New Jersey: Cape May County Chamber of Commerce Bicentennial Commission, 1976.

_____. *A History of Ocean City*. Ocean City, New Jersey: The Friends of the Ocean City Historical Museum, 1965.

_____. *Ocean City Memories*. Ocean City, New Jersey: The Centennial Commission of Ocean City, New Jersey, 1979.

Liebowitz, Steve. *Steel Pier, Atlantic City: Showplace of the Nation*. West Creek, New Jersey: Down The Shore Publishing. 2009.

Lloyd, John Bailey. *Six Miles At Sea: A Pictorial History of Long Beach Island*. Harvey Cedars, New Jersey: Down The Shore Publishing. 1990.

_____. *Eighteen Miles of History on Long Beach Island*. Harvey Cedars, New Jersey: Down The Shore Publishing, 1994.

Loder, Kurt. "A Lake At Sea" in *The Broadsider* [as clipped and filed in the Cape May County Library, Cape May Court House, New Jersey].

McLaughlin, Mark. *Greetings From Ocean City: Historic Postcards From America's Greatest Family Resort*. Harvey Cedars, New Jersey: Down The Shore Publishing. 1995.

McMahon, William. *South Jersey Towns: History and Legend*. New York: Rutgers University Press, 1958.

Moffett, Herbert N. and Cook, Lewis D. *A History of the Somers Mansion*. Atlantic County Historical Society. Somers Point, New Jersey, 1942.

National Audubon Society. *Living With The New Jersey Shore*. Durham, North Carolina: Duke University Press, 1986.

New Jersey Department of Environmental Protection, Division of Coastal Resources. *New Jersey Shore Protection MasterPlan*. Trenton, New Jersey, 1981.

New Jersey Department of Environmental Protection, Division of Water Resources, Bureau of Flood Plain Management. *Coastal Storm Vulnerability Analysis.* Trenton, New Jersey, 1983.

Ocean City Association. *First, Third, Fourth* and *Fifth Annual Reports of the President of the Ocean City Association.* Ocean City, New Jersey, 1881, 1883 and 1885 respectively.

"Ocean City Founded By Ministers" in *The Cape May County Gazette.* June 1942 [as clipped and filed in the Cape May County Library, Cape May Court House, New Jersey].

Ocean City Historical Museum. "The *Sindia* Story: Wreck of the *Sindia.*" Ocean City, New Jersey.

*Polk's Ocean City Directory.* Boston: Polk, 1967.

Reed, Natalie. "Diving the Atlantic Depths" in *The SandPaper,* Ocean City, New Jersey, April 18, 1985.

Rundstrom, Olive Conover. *History of Somers Point.* Atlantic County Historical Society. Pleasantville, New Jersey, 1976.

Rush, Mary Townsend. *Ocean City Guidebook and Directory.* Ocean City, New Jersey: 1892-1895.

Seibold, David J. and Adams, Charles J. III. *Shipwrecks Off Ocean City.* Wyomissing Hills, Pennsylvania: David Seibold, 1986.

Somerville, George B. *The Lure of Long Beach New Jersey.* Harvey Cedars, New Jersey: Down The Shore Publishing, 1987 [Reprint; originally published 1914].

Turner, James Lincoln. *Seven Superstorms of the Northeast, and Other Blizzards, Hurricanes and Tempests.* West Creek, New Jersey: Down the Shore Publishing. 2005.

Voss, J. Ellis. *Ocean City: An Ecological Analysis of a Satellite Community.* Philadelphia: University of Pennsylvania Press, 1941.

Wilson, Harold F. *The Jersey Shore.* New York: Lewis Historical Publishing Co., Inc., 1953.

*The appeal of the sea and the boardwalk is a constant through the years.*

# *Index*

The late Tim Cain worked as an award-winning reporter, columnist, and editor for most of the local newspapers in the Ocean City area as well as for national and state publications. He was especially masterful at gathering oral histories and writing profiles of local personalities.

He also taught writing at the elementary, secondary, and college level, having worked as an instructor at Temple, Drexel, Stockton, and other universities. He received his B.A. at Penn State, his M.A. from Villanova, and completed doctoral work at Temple University.

Active in social justice causes, he held posts in Amnesty International and other human rights organizations, and — proud of his Irish heritage — he had a passion for Irish history.

Down The Shore Publishing specializes in books, calendars, cards and videos about the Jersey Shore. For a free catalog of all our titles or to be included on our mailing list,
just send us a request:

*Down The Shore Publishing*
*Box 100, West Creek, NJ 08092*

info@down-the-shore.com

**www.down-the-shore.com**